Longman
PHOTO
DICTIONARY

EDICION BILINGÜE EN ESPAÑOL

Marilyn S. Rosenthal   Daniel B. Freeman

Longman

INTRODUCTION INTRODUCCIÓN

EL DICCIONARIO FOTOGRÁFICO LONGMAN presenta un panorama fotográfico de la vida y el lenguaje de América del Norte. Es un libro de vocabulario y práctica conversacional que incluye más de 2,000 vocablos para categorizar más de 80 diferentes voces semánticas. Las fotografías en color reflejan la cultura americana moderna y son presentadas tanto contextualmente (El Comedor) como categóricamente (Las Emociones).

EL DICCIONARIO FOTOGRÁFICO LONGMAN también puede usarse para alfabetizar, jugar a las adivinanzas, practicar la audición, dictar, contar historias, categorizar, realizar prácticas de escritura, hacer composiciones, debatir, o trabajar en grupos. Sin duda, este libro se adapta a la práctica de las cuatro destrezas del lenguaje: audición, oratoria, lectura y escritura en cada unidad y pueden éstas variar enormemente dependiendo del nivel lingüístico y las necesidades del estudiante.

Las lecciones son independientes y no se presentan en orden progresivo. Le animamos a que presente Ud. las lecciones del modo más adecuado a su situación docente. Por ejemplo, se puede agrupar el capítulo de los números con el de dinero y banca, o si lo desea puede introducir el de las habitaciones de la casa con el titulado En el Hogar.

Hemos intentado proporcionar una fuente básica de lengua y cultura que se pueda utilizar en distintos niveles lingüísticos tanto en un texto principal como en uno suplementario. Esperamos que las fotografías le estimulen a Ud. y a sus alumnos y les inciten a sobreactuar y a discutir cada tema. Le agradeceríamos que compartiera sus ideas con nosotros.

Marilyn Rosenthal y Daniel Freeman

Agradecimiento especial
La Dra. Clara V. Velázquez, catedrática y directora del Departmento de Inglés del Hostos College de City University of New York, ha efectuado la revisión de la versión en español de este libro. Le agradecemos su meritoria participación.

CONTENTS CONTENIDO

NUMBERS LOS NÚMEROS 1

TIME LA HORA 2

CALENDAR & HOLIDAYS EL CALENDARIO Y LOS DÍAS FESTIVOS 3

WEATHER & SEASONS EL TIEMPO Y LAS ESTACIONES 4

SHAPES FORMAS Y MEDIDAS 5

MONEY & BANKING DINERO Y BANCA 6

THE WORLD EL MUNDO 7

THE UNITED STATES LOS ESTADOS UNIDOS 9

CANADA CANADÁ 10

THE CITY LA CIUDAD 11

THE SUPERMARKET EL SUPERMERCADO 13

FRUIT FRUTAS 15

VEGETABLES VERDURAS 16

THE MENU EL MENÚ 17

FAST FOODS & SNACKS COMIDA RÁPIDA Y BOCADILLOS 18

THE POST OFFICE LA OFICINA DE CORREOS 19

THE OFFICE LA OFICINA 20

OCCUPATIONS LAS OCUPACIONES 21

THE BODY EL CUERPO 23

COSMETICS & TOILETRIES COSMÉTICOS Y ARTÍCULOS DE TOCADOR 25

ACTION AT HOME EN EL HOGAR 26

ACTION AT THE GYM EN EL GIMNASIO 27

ACTION AT SCHOOL EN EL COLEGIO 28

THE DOCTOR EL DOCTOR 29

THE DENTIST EL DENTISTA 30

THE FAMILY LA FAMILIA 31

EMOTIONS LAS EMOCIONES 32

OPPOSITES OPUESTOS 33

MEN'S WEAR ROPA DE CABALLERO 35

WOMEN'S WEAR ROPA DE SEÑORA 36

MEN'S & WOMEN'S WEAR ROPA MASCULINA Y FEMENINA 37

ACCESSORIES ACCESORIOS 38

HOUSING VIVIENDAS 39

THE BACKYARD & GARDEN EL PATIO Y EL JARDÍN 40

THE LIVING ROOM EL SALÓN 41

THE DINING ROOM EL COMEDOR 42

THE BEDROOM EL DORMITORIO 43

THE BATHROOM EL CUARTO DE BAÑO 44

THE KITCHEN LA COCINA 45

KITCHENWARE UTENSILIOS DE COCINA 46

THE NURSERY EL DORMITORIO DEL BEBÉ 47

THE PLAYGROUND EL PATIO 48

THE LAUNDRY ROOM LA LAVANDERÍA 49

TOOLS LAS HERRAMIENTAS 50

ELECTRONICS APARATOS ELÉCTRICOS 51

CONSTRUCTION CONSTRUCCIÓN 53

LAND & WATER TIERRA Y AGUA 54

THE CAR EL AUTÓMOVIL 55

THE TRAIN, BUS & TAXI EL TREN, EL AÚTOBUS Y EL TAXI 56

ROUTES & ROAD SIGNS CARRETERAS Y SEÑALES DE TRÁFICO 57

THE AIRPORT EL AEROPUERTO 59

THE WATERFRONT EL PUERTO 61

THE BEACH LA PLAYA 62

WATER SPORTS DEPORTES ACUÁTICOS 63

WINTER SPORTS DEPORTES DE INVIERNO 64

SPECTATOR SPORTS DEPORTES PARA ESPECTADORES 65

OTHER SPORTS OTROS DEPORTES 67

ENTERTAINMENT ESPECTÁCULOS 69

MUSICAL INSTRUMENTS INSTRUMENTOS MUSICALES 70

THE ZOO & PETS EL ZOOLÓGICO Y LOS ANIMALES DOMÉSTICOS 71

THE FARM LA GRANJA 73

FISH & SEA ANIMALS ANIMALES ACUÁTICOS 74

BIRDS PÁJAROS 75

INSECTS & RODENTS INSECTOS Y ROEDORES 76

SPACE EL ESPACIO 77

THE MILITARY EL EJÉRCITO 78

HOBBIES & GAMES PASATIEMPOS Y JUEGOS 79

SEWING & SUNDRIES LA COSTURA Y ARTÍCULOS DIVERSOS 80

WORD LIST LISTA DE PALABRAS 81

PHOTO CREDITS RECONOCIMIENTOS POR FOTOGRAFÍAS 91

ACKNOWLEDGEMENTS AGRADECIMIENTOS 93

	English	Español
1	one	uno
2	two	dos
3	three	tres
4	four	cuatro
5	five	cinco
6	six	seis
7	seven	siete
8	eight	ocho
9	nine	nueve
10	ten	diez

	English	Español
11	eleven	once
12	twelve	doce
13	thirteen	trece
14	fourteen	catorce
15	fifteen	quince
16	sixteen	dieciséis
17	seventeen	diecisiete
18	eighteen	dieciocho
19	nineteen	diecinueve
20	twenty	veinte

	English	Español
21	twenty-one	veintiuno
30	thirty	treinta
40	forty	cuarenta
50	fifty	cincuenta
60	sixty	sesenta
70	seventy	setenta
80	eighty	ochenta
90	ninety	noventa
100	one hundred	cien
101	one hundred and one	ciento uno

	English	Español
1,000	one thousand	mil
10,000	ten thousand	diez mil
100,000	one hundred thousand	cien mil
1,000,000	one million	un millón

	English	Español
+	plus	más
−	minus	menos
×	times	multiplicado por
÷	divided by	dividido por
=	equals	igual a

¼
one quarter/one fourth
un cuarto

⅓
one third
un tercio

½
one half
(la) mitad

¾
three quarters/
three fourths
tres cuartos

1
one
uno

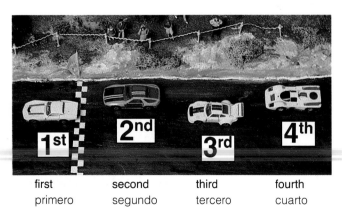

first / primero
second / segundo
third / tercero
fourth / cuarto

100% one hundred percent
100% cien por ciento

10% ten percent
10% diez por ciento

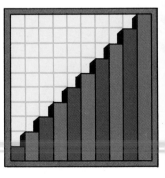

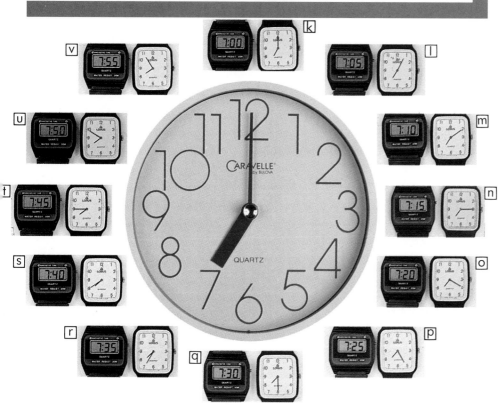

a. **clock**   reloj
b. **hour hand**   horario
c. **minute hand**   minutero
d. **face**   esfera
e. **(digital) watch**   reloj digital
f. **(analog) watch**   reloj analógico
g. **twelve o'clock/midnight**
   las doce en punto | la medianoche
h. **twelve o'clock/noon**
   las doce en punto/el mediodía
i. **eight A.M./eight (o'clock)
   in the morning**
   las ocho de la mañana/
   las ocho (en punto)
j. **eight P.M./eight (o'clock)
   at night**
   las ocho de la tarde/
   las ocho (en punto)
k. **seven o'clock/seven**
   las siete en punto/las siete
l. **seven o five/five after seven**
   las siete y cinco
m. **seven ten/ten after seven**
   las siete y diez
n. **seven fifteen/a quarter
   after seven**
   las siete y cuarto/las siete
   y quince minutos
o. **seven twenty/twenty
   after seven**
   las siete y veinte
p. **seven twenty-five/
   twenty-five after seven**
   las siete y veinticinco
q. **seven thirty/half past seven**
   las siete y treinta minutos/
   las siete y media/
r. **seven thirty-five/twenty five
   to eight**
   las siete y treinta y cinco
   minutos/las ocho menos
   veinticinco
s. **seven forty/twenty to eight**
   las siete y cuarenta minutos/
   las ocho menos veinte
t. **seven forty-five/a quarter to eight**
   las siete y cuarenta y cinco
   minutos/las ocho menos cuarto
u. **seven fifty/ten to eight**
   las siete y cincuenta minutos/
   las ocho menos diez
v. **seven fifty-five/five to eight**
   las siete y cincuenta y cinco
   minutos/las ocho menos cinco

CALENDAR & HOLIDAYS
EL CALENDARIO Y LOS DÍAS FESTIVOS

 1990

A. Year Año

B. Months Meses

January enero
February febrero
March marzo
April abril
May mayo
June junio
July julio
August agosto
September septiembre
October octubre
November noviembre
December diciembre

C. Days of the Week
Días de la Semana

S Sunday
D domingo
M Monday
L lunes
M Tuesday
M martes
W Wednesday
X miércoles
T Thursday
J jueves
F Friday
V viernes
S Saturday
S sábado

D. Holidays
Días Festivos

1. New Year's Day
   El Día de Año Nuevo
2. Valentine's Day
   El Día de San Valentín
3. Washington's Birthday
   El Cumpleaños de Washington
4. St. Patrick's Day
   El Día de San Patricio
5. Easter La Semana Santa
6. Mother's Day
   El Día de la Madre
7. Memorial Day
   El Día de los Caídos por la Patria
8. Father's Day
   El Día del Padre

JANUARY
S M T W T F S
1 2 3 4 5 6
7 8 9 10 11 12 13
14 15 16 17 18 19 20
21 22 23 24 25 26 27
28 29 30 31

FEBRUARY
S M T W T F S
1 2 3
4 5 6 7 8 9 10
11 12 13 14 15 16 17
18 19 20 21 22 23 24
25 26 27 28

MARCH
S M T W T F S
1 2 3
4 5 6 7 8 9 10
11 12 13 14 15 16 17
18 19 20 21 22 23 24
25 26 27 28 29 30 31

APRIL
S M T W T F S
1 2 3 4 5 6 7
8 9 10 11 12 13 14
15 16 17 18 19 20 21
22 23 24 25 26 27 28
29 30

MAY
S M T W T F S
1 2 3 4 5
6 7 8 9 10 11 12
13 14 15 16 17 18 19
20 21 22 23 24 25 26
27 28 29 30 31

JUNE
S M T W T F S
1 2
3 4 5 6 7 8 9
10 11 12 13 14 15 16
17 18 19 20 21 22 23
24 25 26 27 28 29 30

JULY
S M T W T F S
1 2 3 4 5 6 7
8 9 10 11 12 13 14
15 16 17 18 19 20 21
22 23 24 25 26 27 28
29 30 31

AUGUST
S M T W T F S
1 2 3 4
5 6 7 8 9 10 11
12 13 14 15 16 17 18
19 20 21 22 23 24 25
26 27 28 29 30 31

No Holiday

SEPTEMBER
S M T W T F S
1
2 3 4 5 6 7 8
9 10 11 12 13 14 15
16 17 18 19 20 21 22
23 24 25 26 27 28 29
30

OCTOBER
S M T W T F S
1 2 3 4 5 6
7 8 9 10 11 12 13
14 15 16 17 18 19 20
21 22 23 24 25 26 27
28 29 30 31

NOVEMBER
S M T W T F S
1 2 3
4 5 6 7 8 9 10
11 12 13 14 15 16 17
18 19 20 21 22 23 24
25 26 27 28 29 30

DECEMBER
S M T W T F S
1
2 3 4 5 6 7 8
9 10 11 12 13 14 15
16 17 18 19 20 21 22
23 24 25 26 27 28 29
30 31

9. Fourth of July/
   Independence Day
   El Cuatro de julio/Día de la
   Independencia
10. Labour Day
    El Día del Trabajo

11. Halloween
    La Víspera de Todos los Santos
12. Thanksgiving
    El Día de Acción de Gracias
    [en Canadá: 10 de octubre]
13. Christmas La Navidad

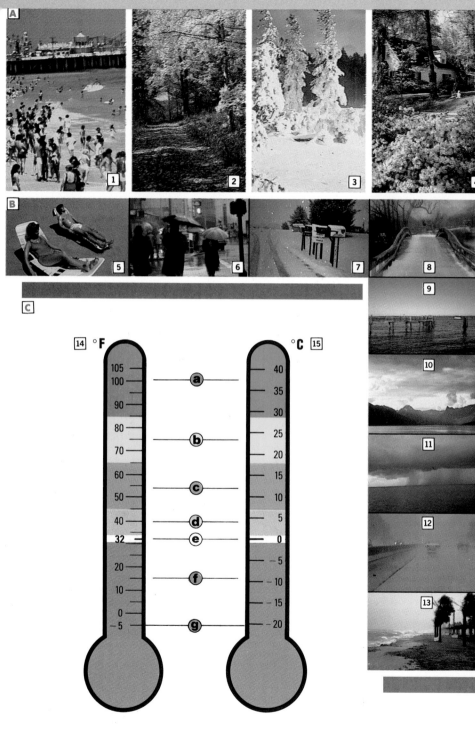

A. Seasons
Las Estaciones del Año

1. summer   el verano
2. fall   el otoño
3. winter   el invierno
4. spring   la primavera

B. Weather
El Tiempo

5. sunny   soleado
6. rainy   lluvioso
7. snowy   nevado
8. icy   helado
9. clear   claro
10. cloudy   nubloso
11. stormy   tormentoso
12. foggy   brumoso
13. windy   ventoso

C. Temperature
La Temperatura

14. degrees Fahrenheit
    grados Fahrenheit
15. degrees Celsius/
    degrees Centigrade
    grados Celsius/
    grados centigrados
    a. hot   calor
    b. warm   buen tiempo
    c. cool/chilly   fresco
    d. cold   frío
    e. freezing   helado
    f. below freezing   bajo cero
    g. five (degrees) below
       (zero)/minus twenty
       (degrees)
       cinco (grados)/veinte (grados)
       bajo cero

SHAPES FORMAS Y MEDIDAS

A. Cube   Cubo

1. corner   esquina
2. top   parte superior
3. front   parte delantera
4. edge   arista
5. depth   profundidad
6. height   altura

B. Isoceles Triangle
Triángulo Isósceles

7. obtuse angle   ángulo obtuso
8. acute angle   ángulo agudo

C. Right Triangle
Triángulo Recto

9. apex   vértice
10. hypotenuse   hipotenusa
11. base   base
12. right angle   ángulo recto

D. Square
Cuadrado

13. side   lado

E. Rectangle
Rectángulo

14. width   anchura
15. length   longitud
16. diagonal   diagonal

F. Circle   Círculo

17. circumference   circunferencia
18. center   centro
19. diameter   diámetro
20. radius   radio

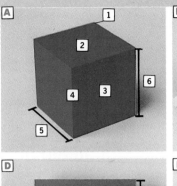

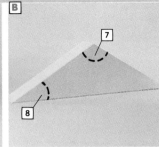

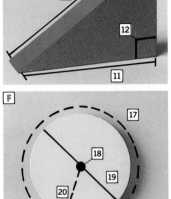

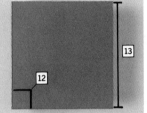

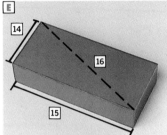

G. Oval/Ellipse
Óvalo/Elipse

H. Cylinder
Cilindro

I. Sphere   Esfera

J. Lines   Líneas

21. perpendicular   perpendicular
22. parallel   paralela
23. spiral   espiral

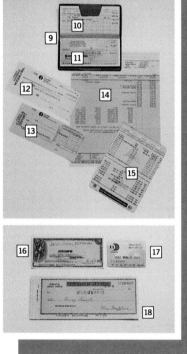

1. **teller** cajero
2. **customer** cliente
3. **bank officer**
   empleado de banca
4. **counter** mostrador
5. **computer** ordenador
6. **bank vault** caja fuerte
7. **safe deposit vault**
   caja de seguridad
8. **cash mashine/**
   automatic teller
   cajero automático
9. **checkbook**
   talonario de cheques
10. **check register/**
    record
    registro de cheques
11. **check** cheque
12. **withdrawal slip**
    justificante de reembolso
13. **deposit slip**
    justificante de depósito
14. **monthly statement**
    estado mensual
15. **bank book**
    cartilla de ahorros
16. **traveler's check**
    cheque de viaje
17. **credit card**
    tarjeta de crédito
18. **money order** orden de pago
19. **penny** penique | centavo
20. **nickel** níquel

21. **dime** dime
22. **quarter** cuarto
23. **half dollar/fifty**
    cent piece
    medio dólar/moneda de
    cincuenta peniques
24. **silver dollar**
    dólar de plata
25. **dollar (bill)/**
    one dollar
    billete de dólar/un dólar
26. **five (dollar bill)/**
    five dollars
    billete de cinco dólares/
    cinco dólares
27. **ten (dollar bill)/**
    ten dollars
    billete de diez dólares/
    diez dólares
28. **twenty (dollar bill)/**
    twenty dollars
    billete de veinte dólares/
    veinte dólares
29. **fifty (dollar bill)/**
    fifty dollars
    billete de cincuenta
    dólares/cincuenta dólares

30. **one hundred**
    (dollar bill)/one
    hundred dollars
    billete de cien dólares/
    cien dólares

THE WORLD   EL MUNDO

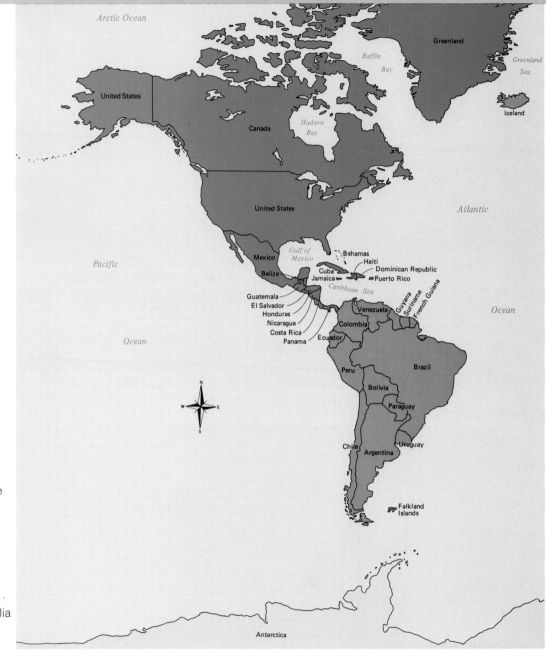

Arctic Ocean

Greenland

Baffin Bay

Greenland Sea

United States

Iceland

Canada

Hudson Bay

Atlantic

United States

Pacific

Gulf of Mexico

Bahamas

Mexico

Haiti

Cuba

Dominican Republic

Belize

Jamaica

Puerto Rico

Caribbean Sea

Ocean

Guatemala

El Salvador

Guyana

Honduras

Venezuela

Suriname

French Guiana

Nicaragua

Colombia

Costa Rica

Ocean

Panama

Ecuador

Brazil

Peru

Bolivia

Paraguay

Chile

Uruguay

Argentina

Falkland Islands

Antarctica

North America
América del Norte
South America
América del Sur
Europe Europa

Asia Asia

Africa África

Australia Australia

Antarctica
Antártida

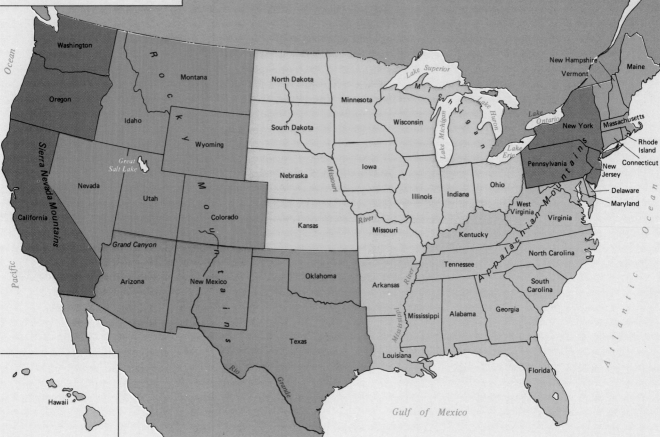

■ New England/The East
Nueva Inglaterra/El Este

■ Middle Atlantic States/The East
Estados del Atlántico Medio/El Este

■ Southern States/The South
Estados del Sur/El Sur

■ Southwestern States/The Southwest
Estados del Suroeste/El Suroeste

■ Midwestern States/The Midwest
Estados del Medio oeste/El Medio oeste

■ Rocky Mountain States
Estados de las Montañas Rocosas

■ Pacific Coast States/The West Coast
Estados de la Costa Pacífica/La Costa del Oeste

N north
N norte
S south
S sur
E east
E este
W west
O oeste

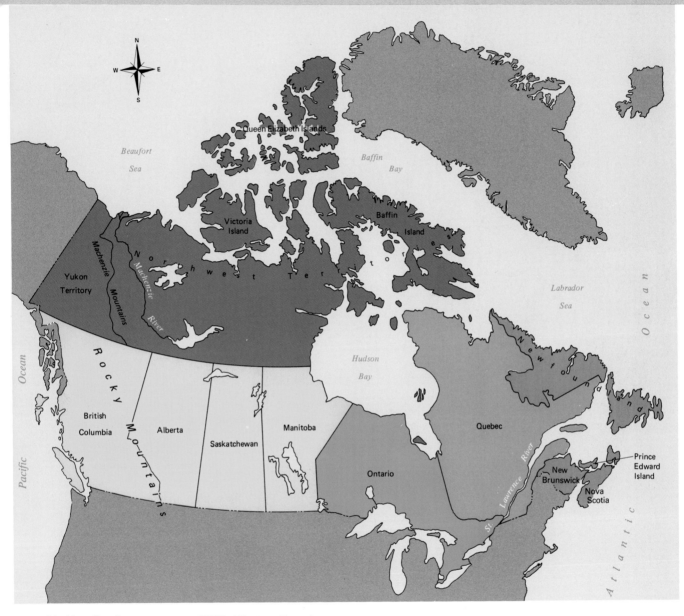

Maritime Provinces
Provincias Marítimas

Quebec Quebec

Ontario Ontario

Western Canada
Canadá Occidental

Northern Canada
Canadá Septentrional

THE CITY LA CIUDAD

1. skyline   horizonte
2. skyscraper   rascacielos
3. fire hydrant   boca de incendios
4. trash can   papelera | basura
5. parking lot   aparcamiento |
   estacionamiento
6. parking meter   parquímetro
7. traffic light   semáforo
8. flag   bandera
9. street   calle
10. crosswalk   paso de peatones
11. pedestrian   peatón
12. bus lane   carril para autobuses
13. (street) corner   esquina
   (de la calle)
14. curb   bordillo
15. phone booth/telephone
   booth   cabina telefónica
16. walk sign   semáforo para
   peatones

17. **one way (traffic) sign** señal (de tráfico) de dirección única
18. **office building** edificio de oficinas
19. **traffic (jam)** (obstrucción de) tráfico
20. **subway (entrance)** la entrada del metro
21. **newsstand** kiosco
22. **street light** farola
23. **bus stop** parada de autobús
24. **street sign** placa de nombre de la calle
25. **bus** autobús
26. **exit** salida
27. **passenger** pasajero
28. **sidewalk** acera

THE SUPERMARKET
EL SUPERMERCADO

A. Check-out Area
Zona de la Caja

1. customer/shopper   cliente
2. cashier   cajera
3. cash register   caja registradora
4. checkbook   talonario
5. groceries   comestibles
6. packer   ayudante de supermercado
7. bag/sack   bolsa
8. check-out counter   mostrador de caja

B. Frozen Foods
Alimentos Congelados

9. frozen vegetables
   verduras congeladas
10. frozen dinner
   comida congelada
11. frozen orange juice
   jugo de naranja congelado

C. Dairy
Productos Lácteos

12. yogurt   yogur
13. cheese   queso
14. eggs   huevos
15. margarine   margarina
16. butter   mantequilla
17. milk   leche

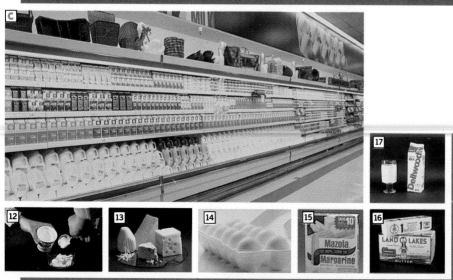

D. Canned Goods
Alimentos Enlatados

18. tuna fish   atún
19. soup   sopa

E. Meat and Poultry
Carne y Aves de Corral

20. bacon   tocino
21. roast   asado
22. pork chops   chuletas de cerdo
23. chicken/roaster   pollo
24. ground meat   carne picada | carne molida
25. steak   filete
26. lamb chops   chuletas de cordero

F. Packaged Goods
Alimentos Envasados

27. bread   pan
28. cereal   cereales
29. cookies   galletas
30. crackers   galletas de aperitivo
31. macaroni   macarrones

1. **apples** manzanas
2. **pears** peras
3. **grapes** uva
4. **kiwis** kiwis
5. **mangoes** mangos
6. **coconuts** cocos
7. **avocados** aguacates
8. **bananas** plátanos
9. **nectarines** nectarinas
10. **plums** ciruelas
11. **cherries** cerezas
12. **apricots** albaricoques
13. **lemons** limones
14. **limes** limas
15. **grapefruits** pomelos
16. **oranges** naranjas
17. **pineapples** piñas
18. **papayas** papayas
19. **peaches** duraznos |
    melocotones
20. **strawberries** fresas
21. **raspberries** frambuesas
22. **blueberries** arándanos
23. **watermelons** sandías
24. **honeydew melons**
    melones dulces
25. **cantaloupes**
    melones de agua

1. **lettuce**   lechuga
2. **green onions/scallions**
   cebolletas
3. **radishes**   rábanos
4. **watercress**   berro
5. **tomatoes**   tomates
6. **cucumbers**   pepinos
7. **celery**   apio
8. **yellow peppers**
   pimientos amarillos
9. **green peppers**
   pimientos verdes
10. **red peppers**
    pimientos rojos
11. **new potatoes**
    patatas nuevas
12. **baking potatoes**
    patatas para asar
13. **sweet potatoes**   boniatos
14. **onions**   cebollas
15. **red onions**   cebollas rojas
16. **pearl onions**
    cebollitas francesas

17. **cauliflower**   coliflor
18. **spinach**   espinacas
19. **garlic**   ajos
20. **artichokes**   alcachofas
21. **green beans/**
    string beans
    judías verdes
22. **eggplants**   berenjenas
23. **carrots**   zanahorias
24. **asparagus**   espárragos
25. **broccoli**   brécol
26. **corn**   maíz
27. **ginger**   jengibre
28. **parsnips**   pastinacas
29. **cabbage**   col
30. **leeks**   puerros
31. **turnips**   nabos
32. **dill**   eneldo

A. Appetizers   Aperitivos

1. tomato juice   jugo de tomate
2. fruit cup/fruit cocktail   macedonia/cóctel de frutas
3. shrimp cocktail   cóctel de gambas

B. Soup and Salad
Sopas y Ensaladas

4. soup   sopa
5. (tossed) salad   ensalada (aliñada)

C. Main Courses/Entrées
Primeros Platos/Entradas

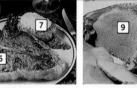

6. steak   filete
7. baked potato   patata asada
8. (dinner) roll   pan
9. roast beef   carne asada
10. stuffed tomatoes   tomates rellenos
11. pork chops   chuletas de cerdo
12. sweet potatoes   boniatos
13. spaghetti and meatballs   espaguetis con albóndigas
14. roast chicken   pollo asado
15. green beans   judías verdes
16. peaches   duraznos | melocotones
17. fish   pescado
18. broccoli   brécol

D. Desserts   Postres

19. apple pie   pastel de manzana
20. chocolate cake   pastel de chocolate
21. ice cream   helado
22. jello   gelatina

E. Beverages   Bebidas

23. coffee   café
24. tea   té

1. hero/submarine sandwich
   sandwich mixto de tamaño grande
2. roast beef sandwich
   sandwich de carne asada
3. pizza   pizza
4. fried squid   calamares fritos
5. fried chicken   pollo frito
6. mustard   mostaza
7. ketchup   catsup
8. relish   salsa
9. pickles   encurtidos
10. onions   cebolla
11. potato chips   patatas fritas
12. tortilla chips
    frituras de maíz
13. pretzels   galletas tostadas
14. popcorn   palomitas de maíz
15. peanuts   cacahuetes
16. candy bar/chocolate
    chocolatina
17. (chewing) gum   chicle
18. donut   donus
19. milk shake   batido
20. soft drink/soda   bebida no alcohólica/refresco
21. straw   sorbete
22. (paper) napkin
    servilleta (de papel)
23. (paper) plate
    plato (de papel)
24. hamburger
    hamburguesa
25. hot dog   perrito caliente
26. onion rings
    aros de cebolla
27. french fries   patatas fritas

THE POST OFFICE
LA OFICINA DE CORREOS

1. postal clerk
   empleado de correos
2. package/parcel   paquete
3. scale   peso
4. express mail
   correo urgente
5. mail slot   buzón
6. mail truck   furgón de
   correos
7. mail carrier   cartero
8. mailbag   cartera
9. mailbox   buzón
10. stamp machine
    máquina expendedora
    de sellos
11. sheet of stamps
    pliego de sellos
12. roll of stamps
    rollo de sellos
13. book of stamps
    carterita de sellos
14. envelope   sobre
15. return address
    señas del remitente
16. address   dirección
17. zip code   código postal
18. stamp   sello
19. (picture) postcard
    postal (con fotografía)
20. return receipt
    acuse de recibo
21. certified mail
    correo certificado

THE OFFICE   LA OFICINA

1. **secretary**   secretaria
2. **(desk) lamp**
   lámpara (de escritorio)
3. **index/file Rolodex**   fichero
4. **pencil holder**   portalápices
5. **(electric) pencil sharpener**
   sacapuntas (eléctrico)
6. **typewriter**   máquina de escribir
7. **typing paper**
   papel de escribir
8. **tape dispenser**   portarrollos
9. **tape/Scotch tape**
   cinta adhesiva
10. **stapler**   grapadora
11. **in box**   bandeja de entrada
12. **out box**   bandeja de salida
13. **paper clip holder**   porta-clip
14. **stationery**   papelería
15. **wastepaper basket**   papelera
16. **file cabinet**   archivador
17. **file folder**   carpeta
18. **bulletin board**
   tablón de anuncios | tabla mural
19. **receptionist**   recepcionista
20. **telephone/switchboard**
   teléfono/centralita
21. **note pad**   libreta de notas
22. **message pad**
   libreta de mensajes
23. **desk calendar**
   calendario de escritorio
24. **desk**   escritorio
25. **(ball point) pen**
   bolígrafo
26. **pencil**   lápiz
27. **eraser**   goma de borrar
28. **rubber band**   goma elástica
29. **paper clip**   clip
30. **staple**   grapa
31. **photocopier/Xerox machine**
   fotocopiadora

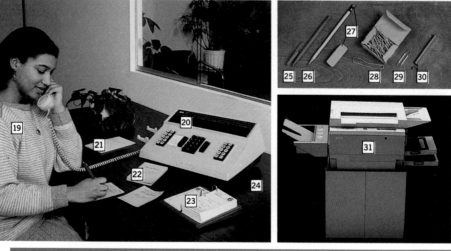

1. construction worker
   obrero de la construcción
2. bricklayer/mason   albañil
3. carpenter   carpintero
4. painter   pintor
5. window washer
   limpiacristales
6. sanitation worker
   basurero
7. truck driver   conductor
   de camión
8. mechanic   mecánico
9. welder   soldador
10. electrician   electricista
11. plumber   fontanero
12. firefighter   bombero
13. police officer   policía
14. mail carrier   cartero
15. fisherman   pescador
16. farmer   granjero
17. florist   florista
18. grocer   tendero
19. butcher   carnicero
20. baker   panadero
21. chef/cook   chef/cocinero
22. waiter   camarero
23. waitress   camarera

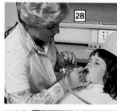
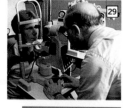

24. **scientist**   científico
25. **doctor/pediatrician**
    doctor/pediatra
26. **nurse**   enfermera
27. **dentist**   dentista
28. **(dental) hygienist**
    higienista (dental)
29. **optometrist**   óptico
30. **veterinarian**   veterinario
31. **pharmacist**   farmacéutico
32. **newscaster**   presentador
33. **journalist**   periodista
34. **computer technician**
    técnico informático
35. **teacher**   profesor
36. **architect**   arquitecto
37. **secretary**   secretaria
38. **teller**   cajero
39. **salesperson**   vendedor
40. **hairdresser**   peluquero
41. **barber**   barbero
42. **tailor**   sastre
43. **seamstress**   costurera
44. **model**   modelo
45. **photographer**   fotógrafo
46. **artist**   artista

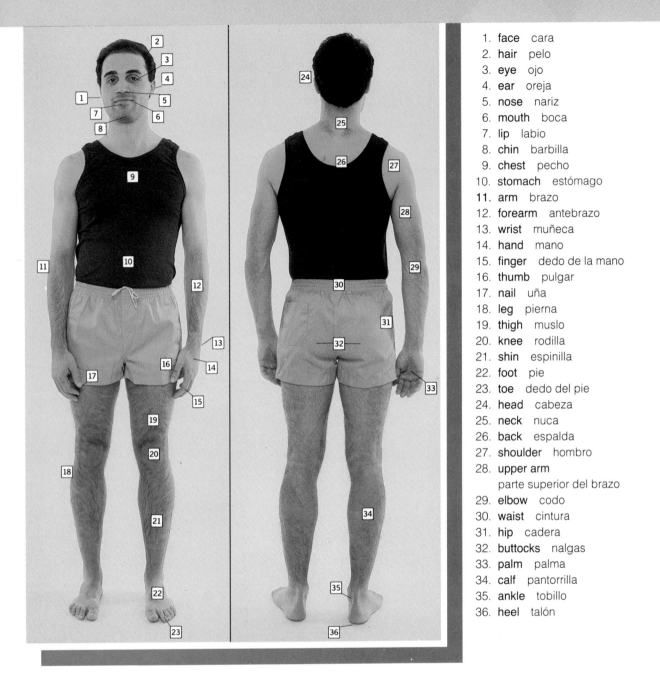

1. **face**   cara
2. **hair**   pelo
3. **eye**   ojo
4. **ear**   oreja
5. **nose**   nariz
6. **mouth**   boca
7. **lip**   labio
8. **chin**   barbilla
9. **chest**   pecho
10. **stomach**   estómago
11. **arm**   brazo
12. **forearm**   antebrazo
13. **wrist**   muñeca
14. **hand**   mano
15. **finger**   dedo de la mano
16. **thumb**   pulgar
17. **nail**   uña
18. **leg**   pierna
19. **thigh**   muslo
20. **knee**   rodilla
21. **shin**   espinilla
22. **foot**   pie
23. **toe**   dedo del pie
24. **head**   cabeza
25. **neck**   nuca
26. **back**   espalda
27. **shoulder**   hombro
28. **upper arm**
    parte superior del brazo
29. **elbow**   codo
30. **waist**   cintura
31. **hip**   cadera
32. **buttocks**   nalgas
33. **palm**   palma
34. **calf**   pantorrilla
35. **ankle**   tobillo
36. **heel**   talón

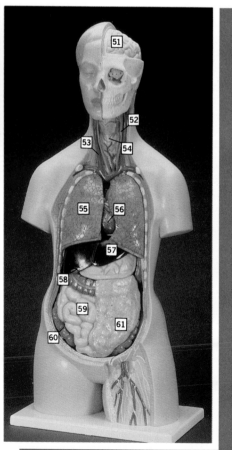

37. **blonde** rubia
38. **brunette** castaña
39. **redhead** pelirroja
40. **forehead** frente
41. **temple** sien
42. **eyebrow** ceja
43. **eyelid** párpado
44. **eyelash** pestaña
45. **pupil** pupila
46. **cheek** mejilla
47. **mustache** bigote
48. **tooth** diente
49. **beard** barba

50. **tongue** lengua
51. **brain** cerebro
52. **artery** arteria
53. **vein** vena
54. **throat** garganta
55. **lung** pulmón
56. **heart** corazón
57. **liver** hígado
58. **gall bladder** vesícula biliar
59. **small intestine** intestino delgado
60. **large intestine** intestino grueso
61. **fatty tissue** tejido adiposo

COSMETICS & TOILETRIES
COSMÉSTICOS Y ARTÍCULOS DE TOCADOR

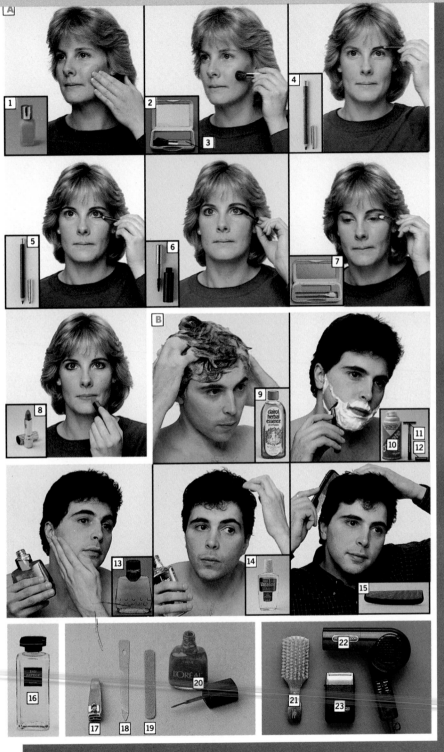

A. Cosmetics
Cosméticos

1. base/foundation   base
2. blush/rouge   colorete
3. brush   brocha
4. eyebrow pencil   lápiz de cejas
5. eyeliner   lápiz de ojos
6. mascara   máscara
7. eye shadow   sombra de ojos
8. lipstick   lápiz de labios | lápiz labia | creyón de labios

B. Toiletries
Artículos de Tocador

9. shampoo   champú
10. shaving cream   crema de afeitar
11. razor   maquinilla de afeitar
12. razor blade   cuchilla
13. after-shave (lotion)   loción para después del afeitado
14. hair tonic   tónico capilar
15. comb   peine
16. cologne   colonia
17. nail clipper   cortauñas
18. nail file   lima de uñas
19. emery board   lima de papel
20. nail polish   esmalte de uñas
21. (hair) brush   cepillo (para el pelo)
22. hair dryer   secador
23. electric shaver   maquinilla eléctrica

ACTION AT HOME EN EL HOGAR

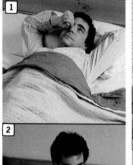

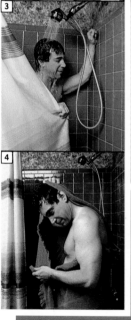

5. **brush your teeth** cepillarse los dientes
6. **shave** afeitarse
7. **get dressed** vestirse

1. **wake up** despertarse
2. **get up** levantarse
3. **take a shower** ducharse
4. **dry off** secarse

8. **wash your face** lavarse la cara
9. **rinse your face** enjuagarse la cara
10. **put on makeup** maquillarse
11. **brush your hair** cepillarse el pelo

12. **cook** cocinar
13. **eat** comer
14. **drink** beber
15. **sweep** barrer
16. **dust** limpiar el polvo
17. **watch (TV)** ver (la TV)
18. **listen** escuchar

19. **take a bath** bañarse
20. **comb your hair** peinarse
21. **go to bed** ir a la cama
22. **sleep** dormir

1. **bend**   doblarse
2. **stretch**   estirarse
3. **sit**   sentarse
4. **lie down**   tumbarse

5. **kneel**   arrodillarse
6. **walk**   andar
7. **hop**   saltar con un pie
8. **run**   correr

9. **swing**   balancearse
10. **reach**   alcanzar
11. **catch**   coger
12. **throw**   lanzar

13. **push**   empujar
14. **lift**   levantar
15. **pull**   tirar
16. **kick**   golpear (con el pie)

1. **write** escribir	13. **draw** dibujar
2. **teach** enseñar	14. **smile** sonreír
3. **erase** borrar	15. **laugh** reír
4. **give** dar	16. **point** señalar
5. **take** coger	17. **touch** tocar
6. **tear up** romper	18. **frown** fruncir
7. **carry** llevar	el ceño | fruncir
8. **read** leer	el entrecejo
9. **pick up** recoger	19. **go up** subir
10. **paint** pintar	20. **wave** saludar
11. **sculpt** modelar	21. **stand** estar de pie
12. **cut** cortar	22. **go down** bajar
	23. **fall** caer

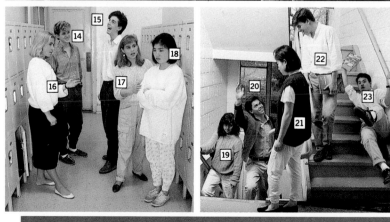

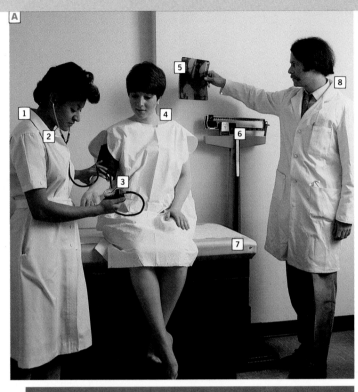

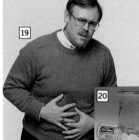

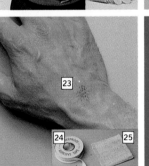

A. The Doctor's Office
La Consulta del Doctor

1. nurse   enfermera
2. stethoscope   estetoscopio
3. blood pressure gauge
   tensiómetro
4. patient   paciente
5. x-ray   radiografía
6. scale   peso
7. examination table
   mesa de reconocimiento
8. doctor   doctor

B. Sickness and Medicine
Enfermedades Y Medicinas

9. headache   dolor de cabeza
10. aspirin   aspirina
11. fever   fiebre
12. thermometer   termómetro
13. cold   resfriado
14. tissue/Kleenex
    pañuelos de papel

15. cold tablets   pastillas antigripales
16. cough   tos
17. cough syrup   jarabe para la tos
18. cough drops   pastillas para la tos
19. stomachache   dolor de estómago
20. antacid/Alka Seltzer   antiácidos/
    Alka Seltzer

21. cut   corte
22. Band-Aid   tirita
23. scratch   arañazo
24. adhesive tape
    esparadrapo
25. bandage/gauze
    venda
26. prescription
    receta médica

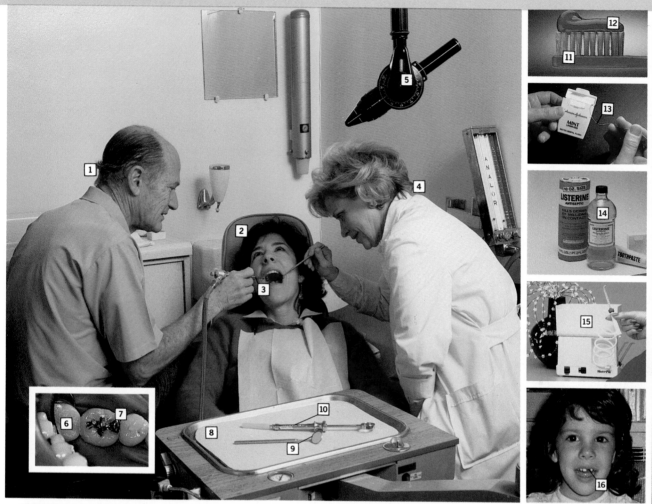

1. **dentist**   dentista
2. **patient**   paciente
3. **drill**   fresa/torno
4. **dental assistant**   asistente dental
5. **x-ray machine**   aparato de rayos X
6. **tooth**   diente
7. **filling**   empaste
8. **tray**   bandeja
9. **mirror**   espejo
10. **Novocain**   Novocaína
11. **toothbrush**   cepillo de dientes
12. **toothpaste**   pasta dentífrica
13. **dental floss**   seda dental
14. **mouthwash**   antiséptico bucal
15. **Water Pik**   equipo de higiene dental de agua a presión
16. **missing tooth**   hueco
17. **braces**   banda/aparato corrector

The Kennedy Family   La Familia Kennedy

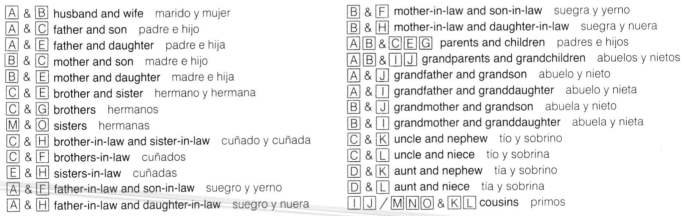

A & B husband and wife marido y mujer
A & C father and son padre e hijo
A & E father and daughter padre e hija
B & C mother and son madre e hijo
B & E mother and daughter madre e hija
C & E brother and sister hermano y hermana
C & G brothers hermanos
M & O sisters hermanas
C & H brother-in-law and sister-in-law cuñado y cuñada
C & F brothers-in-law cuñados
E & H sisters-in-law cuñadas
A & F father-in-law and son-in-law suegro y yerno
A & H father-in-law and daughter-in-law suegro y nuera

B & F mother-in-law and son-in-law suegra y yerno
B & H mother-in-law and daughter-in-law suegra y nuera
AB & CEG parents and children padres e hijos
AB & IJ grandparents and grandchildren abuelos y nietos
A & J grandfather and grandson abuelo y nieto
A & I grandfather and granddaughter abuelo y nieta
B & J grandmother and grandson abuela y nieto
B & I grandmother and granddaughter abuela y nieta
C & K uncle and nephew tío y sobrino
C & L uncle and niece tío y sobrina
D & K aunt and nephew tía y sobrino
D & L aunt and niece tía y sobrina
IJ / MNO & KL cousins primos

EMOTIONS LAS EMOCIONES

1. pleased   contento
2. happy   feliz
3. ecstatic   extático
4. surprised   sorprendido
5. shocked   confundido/ ofendido/escandalizado
6. sad   triste
7. miserable   abatido
8. grieving   afligido
9. displeased   enfadado
10. angry/mad   enojado
11. furious   furioso
12. annoyed   molesto
13. disgusted   disgustado/ asqueado
14. embarrassed   turbado/ avergonzado
15. ashamed   avergonzado
16. nervous   nervioso
17. worried   preocupado
18. scared/afraid   temeroso/ asustado
19. determined   decidido
20. proud   orgulloso
21. smug   presumido
22. shy   tímido
23. bored   aburrido
24. confused   confuso/ confundido
25. suspicious   suspicaz

OPPOSITES OPUESTOS

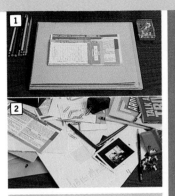

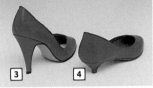

1. **neat** ordenado
2. **messy** desordenado

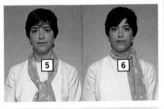

3. **high** alto
4. **low** bajo

5. **loose** flojo
6. **tight** apretado

7. **light** ligero
8. **heavy** pesado

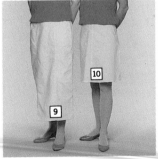

9. **long** largo
10. **short** corto

11. **good** bueno
12. **bad** malo

13. **tall** alto
14. **short** bajo

15. **young** joven
16. **old** viejo

17. **clean** limpio
18. **dirty** sucio

19. **pretty** bonito
20. **ugly** feo

21. **wet** mojado
22. **dry** seco

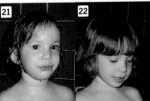

23. **straight** liso
24. **curly** rizado

25. **fast**   rápido
26. **slow**   lento

27. **hot**   caliente
28. **cold**   frío

29. **open**   abierto
30. **closed**   cerrado

31. **full**   lleno
32. **empty**   vacío

33. **new**   nuevo
34. **old**   viejo

35. **light**   claro
36. **dark**   oscuro

37. **straight**   recto
38. **crooked**   torcido

39. **wide**   ancho
40. **narrow**   estrecho

41. **thick**   grueso
42. **thin**   delgado

43. **soft**   blando
44. **hard**   duro

45. **smooth**   suave
46. **rough**   áspero

47. **over**
   sobre/encima de
48. **under**
   debajo de/bajo

A. The Suit
El Traje

1. suit   traje
2. jacket   chaqueta | chaquetón
3. sleeve   manga
4. lapel   solapa
5. shirt   camisa
6. collar   cuello
7. tie   corbata
8. vest   chaleco

B. Casual Wear
Ropa De Sport

9. sport jacket/sport coat   chaqueta de sport
10. pocket   bolsillo
11. sweater   jersey
12. slacks/pants   pantalones
13. sport shirt   camisa deportiva
14. belt   cinturón
15. (belt) buckle   hebilla (de cinturón)
16. jeans   vaqueros | tejanos

C. Underwear
Ropa Interior

17. boxer shorts   calzoncillo
18. briefs/Jockey shorts   slip | refajo
19. sock   calcetín
20. undershirt/t-shirt   camiseta

D. Colors
Colores

21. brown   marrón
22. gray   gris
23. green   verde
24. white   blanco
25. red   rojo
26. tan   crema
27. blue   azul

E. Patterns
Dibujos

28. checked   a cuadros
29. paisley   cachemira
30. solid   liso
31. plaid   escocés
32. striped   a rayas

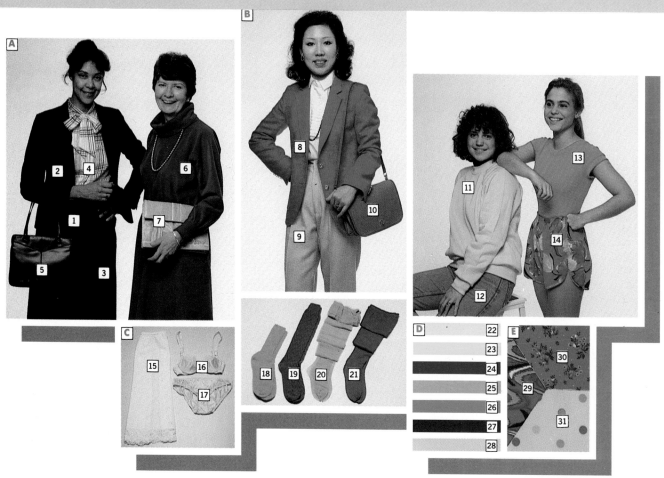

A. The Suit and Dress
El Traje y el Vestido

1. suit traje
2. jacket chaqueta
3. skirt falda
4. blouse blusa
5. handbag bolso
6. dress vestido
7. clutch bag cartera

B. Casual Wear
Ropa de Sport

8. blazer blazer
9. slacks/pants pantalones
10. shoulder bag bandolera
11. sweatshirt suéter
12. jeans vaqueros/tejanos
13. t-shirt camiseta
14. shorts pantalón corto
15. (half) slip combinación
16. bra sujetador | justillo
17. underpants/panties braga

C. Underwear
Ropa Interior

18. sock calcetín
19. knee sock calcetín alto
20. panty hose leotardos
21. tights leotardos

D. Colors
Colores

22. pink rosa
23. yellow amarillo
24. purple púrpura
25. orange naranja
26. turquoise turquesa
27. black negro
28. beige beige

E. Pattern
Dibujos

29. print estampado
30. flowered estampado de flores
31. polka dot estampado de lunares

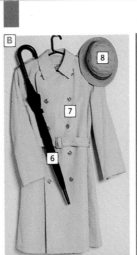

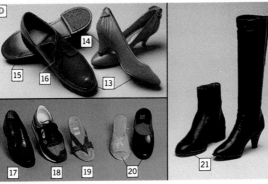

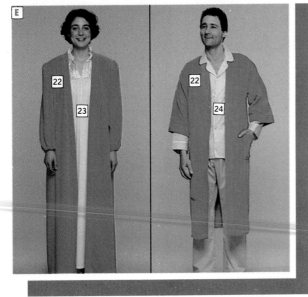

A. Outerwear
Ropa de Abrigo

1. coat   abrigo
2. jacket   cazadora
3. cap   gorra
4. hat   sombrero
5. glove   guante

B. Rainwear
Ropa de Lluvia

6. umbrella   paraguas
7. raincoat/trench coat
   gabardina/impermeable
8. rain hat   sombrero de lluvia

C. Sweaters
Jerseys

9. crewneck   cuello a la caja
10. turtleneck   cuello cisne
11. V-neck   cuello pico
12. cardigan   chaqueta de punto

D. Footwear
Calzado

13. shoe   zapato
14. heel   tacón
15. sole   suela
16. shoelace   cordón
17. loafer   mocasín
18. sneaker   zapatilla deportiva
19. sandal   sandalia
20. slipper   zapatilla
21. boot   bota

E. Nightwear
Ropa de Dormir

22. robe   bata
23. nightgown   camisón
24. pajamas   pijama

ACCESSORIES ACCESORIOS

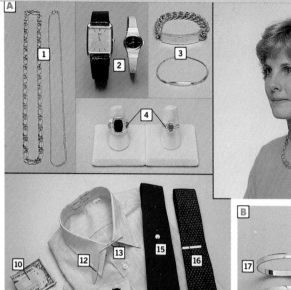

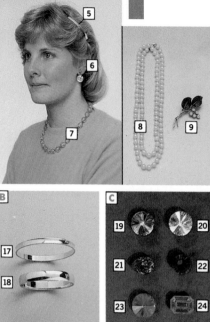

A. Jewelry
Joyería

1. chain   cadena
2. watch   reloj
3. bracelet   brazalete
4. ring   anillo
5. barette   pasador
6. earring   pendiente
7. necklace   collar
8. pearls   perlas
9. pin   broche
10. money clip   portabilletes
11. key ring   llavero
12. stay   ballenas
13. collar bar   alfiler de cuello
14. cuff link   gemelo
15. tiepin/tie tack   alfiler de corbata
16. tie bar/tie clip
    pasador de corbata

B. Metals
Metales

17. gold   oro
18. silver   plata

C. Gems
Piedras Preciosas

19. topaz   topacio
20. diamond   diamante
21. amethyst   amatista
22. ruby   rubí
23. sapphire   zafiro
24. emerald   esmeralda

D. Accessories
Accesorios

25. briefcase   maletín
26. tote bag   bolso
27. attaché case   portafolios
28. change purse   monedero
29. wallet   billetera
30. scarf   bufanda
31. handkerchief   pañuelo

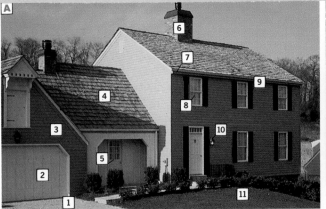

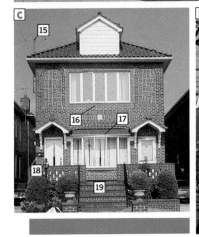

A. Two-Story House
Casa de Dos Plantas

1. driveway   entrada de vehículos
2. garage door   puerta de garaje
3. garage   garaje
4. roof   tejado
5. side door   puerta lateral
6. chimney   chimenea
7. gutter   cangilón
8. window   ventana
9. shutter   contraventana
10. (porch) light   luz (del porche)
11. lawn   césped

B. Ranch House
Casa de Una Planta

12. front walk   acceso de entrada
13. doorknob   pomo
14. front door   puerta principal

C. Two-Family House/Duplex
Casa Para Dos Familias

15. antenna   antena
16. upstairs apartment   apartamento en planta superior

17. downstairs apartment   apartamento en planta inferior/planta baja
18. mailbox   buzón
19. (front) steps   escalera (de acceso)

D. Apartment Building
Edificio de Apartamentos

20. lobby   recibidor
21. elevator   ascensor
22. first floor   primera planta
23. second floor   segunda planta
24. balcony   terraza

E. Floor Plan
Plano de Distribución

25. hall/corridor   recibidor/corredor/pasillo
26. kitchen   cocina
27. bathroom   cuarto de baño
28. dining room   comedor
29. closet   armario
30. living room   salón
31. bedroom   dormitorio

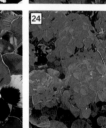

1. tree   árbol
2. leaf   hoja
3. lawn/grass   césped/hierba
4. lawn mower   cortacésped
5. lounge chair   tumbona
6. wading pool   piscina infantil
7. barbecue   barbacoa
8. patio   patio
9. umbrella   sombrilla
10. (patio) table   mesa (de jardín)
11. (patio) chair   silla (de jardín)
12. bush   arbusto
13. flower bed   macizo

14. hedge   seto
15. vegetable garden   huerta
16. watering can   regadera
17. rake   rastrillo
18. trowel   desplantador
19. rose   rosa
20. daisy   margarita
21. azalea   azalea
22. snapdragon   boca de dragón
23. pansy   pensamiento
24. geranium   geranio
25. tulip   tulipán
26. daffodil   narciso

1. **couch/sofa**   tresillo/sofá
2. **cushion**   almohadón
3. **(throw) pillow**   almohada
4. **club chair**   sillón
5. **love seat**   canapé
6. **coffee table**   mesa baja
7. **end table**   mesita rinconera
8. **lamp**   lámpara
9. **lamp shade**   tulipa
10. **wall unit**   módulo de pared
11. **bookcase**   librería

12. **book**   libro
13. **window**   ventana
14. **drape**   cortina
15. **plant**   planta
16. **planter**   tiesto
17. **flowers**   flores
18. **vase**   jarrón
19. **fireplace**   hogar de chimenea
20. **(fireplace) screen**   rejilla (de chimenea)
21. **mantel**   repisa
22. **picture**   cuadro

23. **(picture) frame**
    marco (de cuadro)
24. **side table**   aparador
25. **ottoman**   otomana
26. **rug**   alfombra
27. **floor**   suelo
28. **ceiling**   techo

1. centerpiece   centro
2. wine glass   copa de vino
3. water glass   copa de agua
4. napkin ring   servilletero
5. napkin   servilleta
6. plate   plato
7. (dining room) table
   mesa (del comedor)
8. chair   silla
9. armchair   silla de cabecera
10. (salad) fork
    tenedor (primer plato)
11. (dinner) fork
    tenedor (segundo plato)
12. knife   cuchillo
13. soupspoon   cuchara
14. teaspoon   cucharilla
15. (serving) bowl
    sopera (de servir)
16. server   pala
17. cup   taza
18. saucer   platillo
19. teapot   tetera
20. sideboard/buffet   aparador
21. mirror   espejo
22. chandelier   candelabro

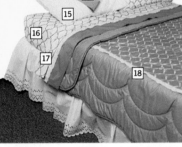

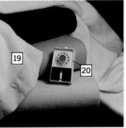

1. **night table/nightstand** mesilla
2. **headboard** cabecera
3. **throw pillow** cojín
4. **bed** cama
5. **bedspread** edredón
6. **dust ruffle** faldillas
7. **carpet** alfombra
8. **lamp** lámpara
9. **chest (of drawers)** cómoda
10. **drawer** cajón
11. **handle/pull** tirador
12. **mirror** espejo
13. **dresser** tocador
14. **pillowcase** funda de almohada
15. **pillow** almohada
16. **(fitted) sheet** sábana bajera
17. **(flat) sheet** sábana encimera
18. **comforter/quilt** colcha
19. **electric blanket** manta eléctrica
20. **(heat) control** control (del calentador)
21. **mattress** colchón
22. **box spring** canapé

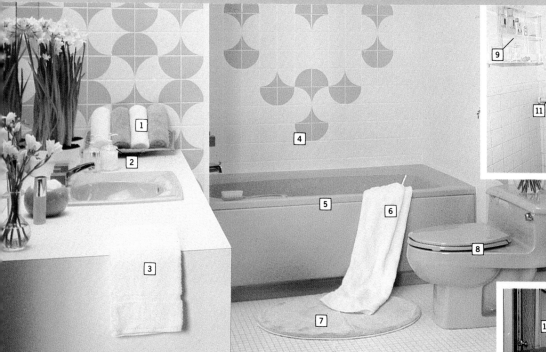

1. **guest towel** toalla para invitados
2. **soap dispenser** jabonera
3. **hand towel** toalla de manos
4. **tile** azulejo
5. **bathtub/tub** bañera
6. **bath towel** toalla de baño
7. **bath mat/bath rug** alfombra
8. **toilet** retrete
9. **shelf** estante
10. **light switch** interruptor de luz
11. **towel rack** toallero
12. **doorknob** pomo de puerta
13. **toilet paper** papel higiénico
14. **mirror** espejo
15. **medicine cabinet** armarito
16. **cup** taza
17. **toothbrush** cepillo de dientes
18. **toothbrush holder** portacepillo de dientes
19. **soap** jabón
20. **soap dish** jabonera
21. **sink** lavamanos
22. **hot water faucet** grifo de agua caliente
23. **cold water faucet** grifo de agua fría
24. **shower head** ducha
25. **shower curtain rod** barra de cortinilla de ducha
26. **shower curtain** cortinilla de ducha
27. **washcloth** manopla

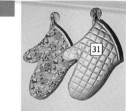

1. **oven** horno	13. **stove/range** cocina	26. **cutting board** tabla para cortar
2. **spice rack** especiero	14. **burner** quemador	27. **(paring) knife** cuchillo (de mondar)
3. **spices** especias	15. **(copper) pot** cazo (de cobre)	28. **dish towel** trapo de cocina
4. **canister** tarro	16. **coffee pot** cafetera	29. **Saran wrap/plastic wrap** plástico para envolver
5. **trivet** salvamanteles	17. **creamer** lechera	
6. **sink** fregadero	18. **cup** taza	
7. **faucet** grifo	19. **saucer** platillo	30. **aluminium foil** aluminio doméstico
8. **cake stand** bandeja para tartas	20. **counter** mostrador	31. **pot holder** manopla
9. **cookbook** libro de cocina	21. **bowl** tazón	
	22. **plate** plato	
10. **freezer** congelador	23. **drawer** cajón	
11. **refrigerator** nevera	24. **cupboard/cabinet** armario	
12. **dishwasher** lavavajillas	25. **(door) handle** tirador (de puerta)	

KITCHENWARE
UTENSILIOS DE COCINA

1. double boiler
   cazo doble | baño de María
2. lid/cover   tapa
3. pot   cazo
4. casserole   cacerola
5. frying pan/skillet   sartén
6. handle   asa
7. roaster   cazuela para asar
8. cake pan   molde para tartas
9. bowl   palangana
10. cookie sheet   bandeja
    de horno
11. rolling pin   rodillo
12. measuring cup   jarra de
    medidas
13. measuring spoon
    cuchara de medidas
14. coffee maker   cafetera
15. microwave oven
    horno microondas
16. can opener   abrelatas
17. blender   batidora
18. food processor   robot
19. toaster oven
    horno para asar
20. (electric) mixer
    mezcladora (eléctrica)
21. toaster   tostadora
22. ladle   cazo
23. (hand) beater/egg
    beater
    batidora (de huevos)
24. knife   cuchillo
25. strainer   colador
26. garlic press
    triturador de ajos
27. grater   rallador
28. whisk   batidor
29. bottle opener
    abrebotellas
30. peeler   pelador
31. spatula   espátula

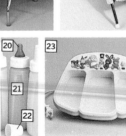

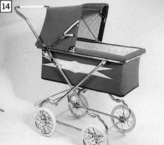

1. **changing pad**
   almohadilla
2. **child** niño
3. **bar** barandilla
4. **crib** cuna
5. **chest (of drawers)** cómoda
6. **lamp** lámpara
7. **teddy bear**
   osito de peluche
8. **stuffed animal** animal
   de peluche
9. **baby chair** silla
10. **rug** alfombra
11. **stroller** cochecito
12. **baby/infant** bebé/niño
13. **baby carrier**
    mochila portabebé
14. **carriage** cochecito
15. **car seat** asiento para coche
16. **highchair** trona
17. **playpen** parque | playpen
18. **baby seat**
    asiento para niño
19. **bib** babero
20. **nipple** tetina
21. **(baby) bottle** biberón
22. **cap/top** tapón
23. **food warmer**
    calienta comida
24. **(baby) clothes**
    ropa (infantil)
25. **diaper** pañal

1. see-saw/teeter-totter
   balancín
2. slide tobogán
3. toddler/child niño
4. tricycle triciclo
5. swing columpio
6. bench banco
7. jungle gym laberinto
8. sandbox fosa de arena
9. sand arena
10. pail cubo

11. shovel pala
12. overalls mono
13. sneakers
    zapatillas
14. water fountain
    fuente
15. doll muñeca
16. doll carriage
    cochecito de
    muñecas
17. skateboard
    monopatín
18. kite cometa

THE LAUNDRY ROOM
LA LAVANDERÍA

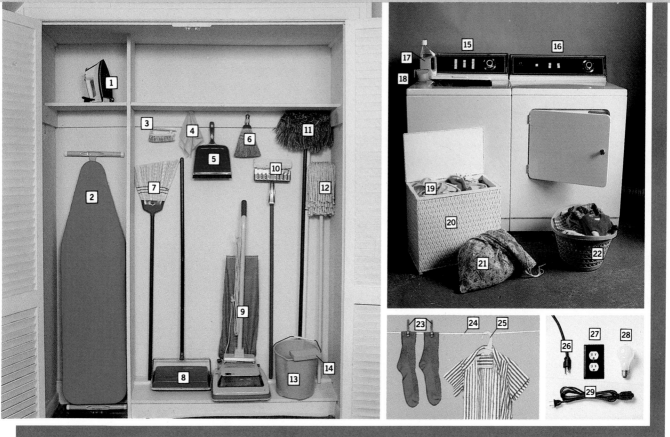

1. iron plancha
2. ironing board tabla de planchar
3. scrub brush cepillo de raíces
4. dust cloth gamuza para el polvo
5. dustpan recogedor
6. whisk broom escobilla
7. broom escoba
8. carpet sweeper
   cepillo para alfombras
9. vacuum cleaner aspiradora
10. (sponge) mop
    mopa (con esponja)
11. (dust) mop
    mopa (para el polvo)
12. (wet) mop fregona
13. bucket/pail cubo
14. sponge esponja
15. washer/washing machine lavadora
16. dryer secadora
17. detergent detergente
18. measuring cup medida
19. laundry ropa sucia
20. hamper canasta
21. laundry bag
    saco de ropa sucia
22. laundry basket
    cesto de ropa sucia
23. clothespin pinza
24. clothesline cuerda
25. hanger percha
26. three-pronged plug
    enchufe de tres clavijas
27. (wall) socket/outlet
    enchufe
28. bulb bombilla
29. extension cord alargadera

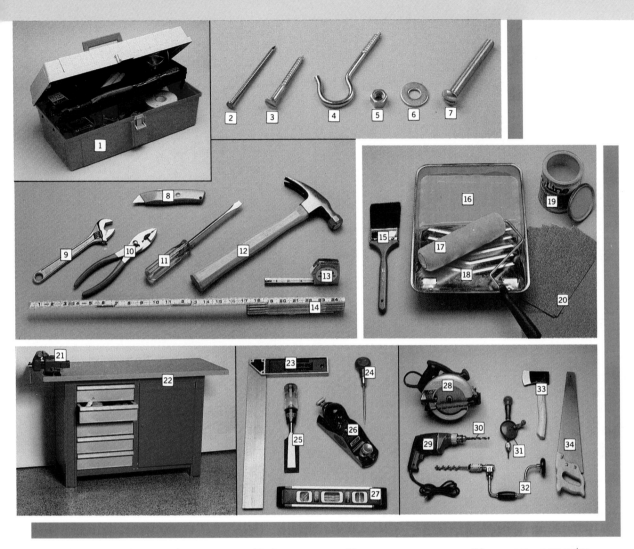

1. **toolbox**   caja de herramientas
2. **nail**   clavo
3. **screw**   tornillo
4. **hook**   escarpia
5. **nut**   tuerca
6. **washer**   arandela
7. **bolt**   perno
8. **utility knife**   navajilla
9. **wrench**   llave inglesa
10. **pliers**   alicates
11. **screwdriver**   destornillador

12. **hammer**   martillo
13. **tape measure**   cinta métrica
14. **folding rule**   metro de carpintero
15. **paintbrush/brush**   brocha
16. **paint**   pintura
17. **(paint) roller**
    rodillo (de pintar)
18. **pan**   cazoleta
19. **(paint) can**   lata (de pintura)
20. **sandpaper**   lija
21. **vise**   tornillo de banco
22. **workbench**   banco de trabajo

23. **square**   escuadra
24. **awl**   lezna
25. **chisel**   formón
26. **plane**   cepillo
27. **level**   nivel
28. **power saw**
    sierra eléctrica
29. **electric drill**
    taladradora eléctrica
30. **bit**   broca
31. **hand drill**
    taladrador manual
32. **brace**   berbiquí
33. **hatchet**   hacha
34. **saw**   sierra

1. **video cassette recorder/VCR**
   videocasete
2. **(video) cassette**   cinta
   (de video)
3. **remote control**   mando a distancia
4. **television/TV**   televisión
5. **screen**   pantalla
6. **stereo system**   equipo estéreo
7. **record**   disco
8. **turntable**   giradiscos/plato
9. **amplifier**   amplificador
10. **tuner**   sintonizador
    de radio/radio
11. **tape deck/cassette deck**
    platina

12. **speaker**
    altavoz | bocina | altoparlante
13. **compact disc player**
    reproductor de compact disc
14. **compact disc/CD**
    compact disc | disco compacto
15. **radio**   radio
16. **clock radio**   despertador
    con radio
17. **tape recorder/cassette player**
    magnetófono/grabadora
18. **personal cassette player/Walkman**
    walkman
19. **headphone**   auricular
20. **(audio) cassette/tape**   cinta/casete
21. **answering machine**   contestador
    automático
22. **telephone**   teléfono

23. **computer**   ordenador
24. **display screen/monitor**
    pantalla/monitor
25. **floppy disc/diskette**
    disco blando/diskete
26. **keyboard**   teclado
27. **printer**   impresora
28. **pocket calculator**
    calculadora de bolsillo
29. **calculator**   calculadora
30. **tape**   rollo
31. **adapter**   adaptador de corriente
32. **battery**   pila
33. **voltage converter**   transformador

34. **plug converter**
    adaptador de clavija
35. **electronic typewriter**
    máquina de escribir electrónica
36. **electric typewriter**
    máquina de escribir eléctrica
37. **disc camera**
    cámara fotográfica de disco
38. **disc film**   película de disco
39. **camera**   cámara fotográfica
40. **lens**   lente
41. **flash**   flash
42. **film**   película
43. **video camera**   cámara de vídeo
44. **slide projector**   proyector de
    diapositivas

1. **construction worker**
   obrero de la construcción
2. **hook** gancho
3. **girder** viga
4. **ladder** escalera
5. **hard hat** casco
6. **tool belt**
   cinturón para herramientas
7. **scaffold** andamio
8. **crane** grúa
9. **excavation site**
   excavación
10. **dump truck**
    camión volquete
11. **frontend loader**
    pala excavadora
12. **backhoe**
    tractor excavador
13. **blasting mat**
    escombros
14. **cement mixer**
    hormigonera
15. **cement** cemento
16. **trowel** llana
17. **brick** ladrillo
18. **level** nivel
19. **wheelbarrow** carretilla
20. **jack hammer/ pneumatic drill**
    martillo neumático
21. **shovel** pala
22. **sledge hammer** mazo
23. **pickaxe** pico

1. **mountain** montaña
2. **peak** pico | cumbre
3. **meadow** pradera
4. **valley** valle
5. **hill** colina
6. **tree** árbol
7. **grass** hierba
8. **field** campo
9. **cliff** acantilado
10. **rock** roca
11. **forest** bosque
12. **lake** lago
13. **pond** estanque
14. **river** río
15. **stream/brook** arroyo
16. **waterfall** cascada
17. **desert** desierto
18. **dune** duna

1. **gas station**   gasolinera
2. **gas pump**   surtidor de gasolina
3. **nozzle**   boquilla
4. **hose**   manguera
5. **attendant**   ayudante
6. **(rear) windshield**
   parabrisas (trasero)
7. **trunk**   capó | cajuela | baúl
8. **license plate**   matrícula
9. **taillight**   intermitente
10. **bumper**   parachoques
11. **steering wheel**   volante
12. **windshield wiper**
   limpiaparabrisas/escobilla
13. **dashboard/**
   instrument panel
   panel de instrumentos

14. **speedometer**
   velocímetro/cuentakilómetros
15. **fuel gauge**
   indicador de gasolina
16. **temperature gauge**
   indicador de temperatura
17. **turn signal**
   palanca de intermitencia
18. **ignition**   encendido
19. **heater**   calefacción
20. **clutch**   embrague
21. **brake**   freno
22. **gas pedal/accelerator**
   acelerador
23. **gearshift**   caja de cambios/
   palanca de cambios
24. **seat**   asiento
25. **heater hose**   manguito
   de calefacción

26. **air filter**   filtro de aire
27. **battery**   batería
28. **engine**   motor
29. **alternator**   alternador
30. **cool air duct**   manguito
   de aire frío
31. **coolant recovery tank**
   depósito de expansión de refrigerante
32. **radiator**   radiador
33. **sedan**   sedán
34. **hubcap**   tapacubos
35. **tire**   rueda
36. **convertible**   descapotable
37. **station wagon**   ranchera
38. **pick-up truck**   furgoneta | camioneta

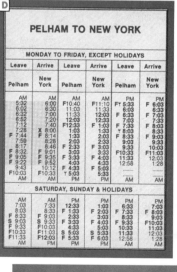

A. The Train Station
La Estación de Ferrocarril

1. information booth   mostrador de información
2. clock   reloj
3. ticket counter   mostrador de billetes
4. arrival and departure board
   tablero de llegadas y salidas
5. train   tren
6. track   vía
7. platform   andén
8. passenger car   vagón de pasajeros
9. porter/redcap   mozo de estación
10. passenger   pasajero

B. The Bus Station
La Estación de Autobuses

11. bus   autobús
12. driver   conductor

13. suitcase   maleta
14. luggage compartment
    compartimento para equipaje

C. The Taxi Stand
La Parada de Taxis

15. taxi   taxi
16. radio call sign
    letrero de llamada por radio
17. off-duty sign
    indicador de fuera de servicio
18. (door) handle
    tirador (de puerta)
19. door   puerta

D. Schedule
Horario

PELHAM TO NEW YORK					
MONDAY TO FRIDAY, EXCEPT HOLIDAYS					
Leave	Arrive	Leave	Arrive	Leave	Arrive
Pelham	New York	Pelham	New York	Pelham	New York
AM	AM	AM	AM	PM	PM
5:32	6:00	F10:40	F11:10	FT 5:33	F 6:03
6:02	6:30	11:03	11:33	6:03	6:33
6:32	7:00	11:33	12:03	F 6:33	F 7:03
6:52	7:20	12:03	12:33	7:03	7:33
7:12	7:40	F12:33	F 1:03	F 7:33	F 8:03
7:28	X 8:00	1:03	1:33	T 8:03	8:33
F 7:44	F 8:14	1:33	2:03	F 8:33	F 9:03
7:59	8:28	2:03	2:33	9:03	9:33
8:17	8:46	F 2:33	F 3:03	9:33	10:03
F 8:32	F 9:01	3:03	3:33	F10:33	F11:03
F 9:05	F 9:35	F 3:33	F 4:03	11:33	12:03
F 9:22	F 9:52	4:03	4:33	12:58	1:28
9:43	10:12	F 4:33	F 5:03		
F10:03	F10:33	T 5:03	5:33		
AM	AM	PM	PM	AM	AM
SATURDAY, SUNDAY & HOLIDAYS					
AM	AM	PM	PM	PM	PM
7:03	7:33	12:33	1:03	6:33	7:03
8:03	8:33	F 1:33	F 2:03	F 7:33	F 8:03
F 8:33	F 9:03	2:33	3:03	8:33	9:03
S 9:03	S 9:33	F 3:33	F 4:03	F 9:33	F10:03
F 9:33	10:03	4:33	5:03	10:33	11:03
F10:33	F11:03	S 5:03	S 5:33	11:33	12:03
F11:33	F12:03	F 5:33	6:03	12:58	1:28
AM	PM	PM	PM	AM	AM

A. Highway
Autopista

1. overpass   paso superior
2. underpass   paso inferior
3. broken line   línea discontinua
4. solid line   línea continua
5. shoulder   arcén
6. divider   mediana
7. left lane   carril izquierdo
8. middle lane   carril central
9. right lane   carril derecho
10. van   furgoneta
11. car   automóvil/coche/carro
12. bus   autobús
13. truck   camión

B. Tollgate   Peaje

14. tollbooth   cabina de peaje
15. exact change lane
    fila de importe exacto
16. change lane   fila de cambio

C. Tunnel   Túnel

17. street light   farola

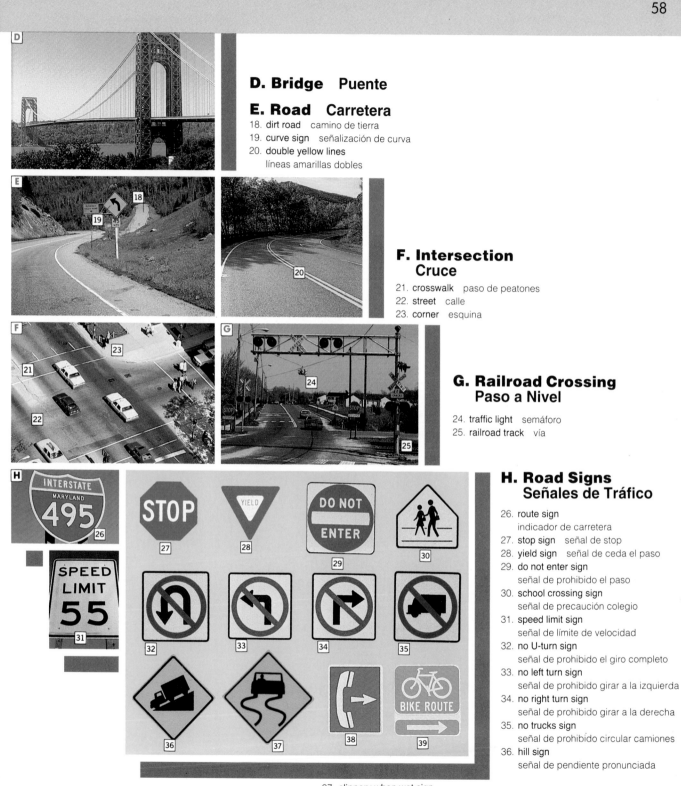

D. Bridge Puente

E. Road Carretera
18. dirt road camino de tierra
19. curve sign señalización de curva
20. double yellow lines
    líneas amarillas dobles

F. Intersection
Cruce
21. crosswalk paso de peatones
22. street calle
23. corner esquina

G. Railroad Crossing
Paso a Nivel
24. traffic light semáforo
25. railroad track vía

H. Road Signs
Señales de Tráfico
26. route sign
    indicador de carretera
27. stop sign señal de stop
28. yield sign señal de ceda el paso
29. do not enter sign
    señal de prohibido el paso
30. school crossing sign
    señal de precaución colegio
31. speed limit sign
    señal de límite de velocidad
32. no U-turn sign
    señal de prohibido el giro completo
33. no left turn sign
    señal de prohibido girar a la izquierda
34. no right turn sign
    señal de prohibido girar a la derecha
35. no trucks sign
    señal de prohibido circular camiones
36. hill sign
    señal de pendiente pronunciada
37. slippery when wet sign
    señal de peligro deslizamiento con
    carretera mojada
38. telephone sign
    señal de teléfono
39. bike route sign
    señal de vía para bicicletas

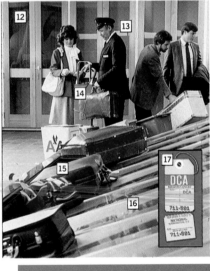

A. The Terminal
La Terminal

1. ticket agent   expendedor de billetes
2. ticket counter   mostrador de billetes
3. suitcase   maleta
4. arrival and departure board   tablero de llegadas y salidas
5. security check   control de seguridad
6. security guard   guardia de seguridad
7. gate   puerta
8. check-in counter   mostrador de facturación
9. waiting room   sala de espera
10. ticket   billete
11. boarding pass   tarjeta de embarque
12. baggage claim area   zona de recogida de equipajes
13. porter/skycap   portero/mozo
14. luggage carrier   carro para equipajes
15. luggage   equipaje
16. (luggage) carousel   cinta transportadora (de equipajes)
17. (baggage) claim check   etiqueta de facturación (de equipaje)
18. customs   aduana
19. customs officer   oficial de aduana
20. documents   documentos
21. passport   pasaporte

B. On Board
A Bordo

22. cockpit   cabina
23. pilot/captain   piloto/comandante
24. co-pilot   copiloto
25. instrument panel   panel de instrumentos
26. cabin   cabina de pasajeros
27. overhead (luggage) compartment   compartimento para equipajes
28. carry-on luggage/carry-on bag   equipaje de mano
29. passenger   pasajero
30. window   ventanilla
31. window seat   asiento de ventanilla
32. middle seat   asiento central
33. aisle seat   asiento de pasillo
34. flight attendant   azafata | aeromoza
35. tray table   mesa abatible
36. tray   bandeja
37. armrest   apoyabrazos

C. The Runway
La Pista de Despegue

38. terminal   terminal
39. jet (plane)   (avión a reacción) jet
40. tail   cola
41. jet engine   motor a reacción
42. wing   ala
43. runway   pista
44. control tower   torre de control
45. rotor   rotor
46. helicopter   helicóptero
47. hangar   hangar

1. harbor   puerto
2. pier/dock   muelle
3. passenger ship/ocean liner
   barco de pasajeros
4. port   babor
5. starboard   estribor
6. bow   proa
7. stern   popa
8. cargo ship/freighter   barco
   de mercancías/carguero
9. cargo   carga
10. deck   cubierta
11. winch   cabrestante
12. line   soga
13. derrick   pluma
14. dock worker/longshoreman
    trabajador portuario
15. crane   grúa
16. (oil) tanker   petrolero
17. buoy   boya
18. barge   barcaza/gabarra
19. tugboat   remolcador
20. ferry   ferry

THE BEACH LA PLAYA

1. hotel hotel
2. boardwalk paseo marítimo | malecón
3. sand arena
4. (beach) blanket manta (playera)
5. (beach) towel toalla (playera)
6. trash can papelera
7. (beach) chair silla (playera)
8. (beach) umbrella sombrilla (playera)
9. lounge chair tumbona
10. lifeguard stand silla del salvavidas
11. lifeguard salvavidas
12. wave ola
13. ocean océano
14. (beach) ball balón (playero)
15. (beach) hat/sun hat sombrero (playero)
16. sand castle castillo de arena
17. bathing suit bañador
18. pail/bucket cubo
19. seashell concha
20. rock piedra

WATER SPORTS
DEPORTES ACUÁTICOS

A. Swimming
Natación
1. swimmer nadador
2. swimming pool piscina

B. Diving
Salto
3. diver saltador
4. diving board trampolín

C. Snorkeling
Buceo Recreativo
5. snorkeler buzo con esnórkel
6. snorkel esnórkel

D. Scuba Diving
Pesca Submarina
7. scuba diver buzo
8. wet suit traje de buzo

9. (air) tank bombona (de oxígeno)
10. mask gafas

E. Fishing
Pesca
11. fisherman pescador
12. fishing rod caña de pescar
13. (fishing) line hilo (de pescar)/sedal

F. Surfing
Surf
14. surfer surfista
15. surf oleaje
16. surfboard tabla

G. Windsurfing
Windsurf
17. windsurfer windsurfista
18. sail vela

H. Sailing
Vela
19. sailboat velero
20. mast mástil

I. Waterskiing
Esquí Acuático
21. waterskier esquiador acuático
22. water ski esquí acuático
23. towrope cable de remolque
24. motorboat fueraborda

J. Rowing
Remo
25. rower remero
26. rowboat bote de remos
27. oar remo

K. Canoeing
Piragüismo
28. canoeist piragüista
29. canoe piragua
30. paddle pala

L. Kayaking
Kayac
31. kayaker remero de kayac
32. kayak kayac

M. White Water Rafting
Descenso en Balsa
33. raft balsa
34. life jacket chaleco salvavidas
35. rapids rápidos

A. Sledding   Trineo
1. sled   trineo

B. Downhill Skiing Descenso
2. skier   esquiador
3. pole   bastón
4. (ski) boot   bota (de esquí)
5. ski   esquí
6. chair lift   remonte

C. Cross Country Skiing Esquí de Fondo
7. skier   esquiador
8. ski cap   gorro de esquiar
9. trail   pista

D. Figure Skating Patinaje Artístico sobre Hielo
10. figure skater   patinadora
11. figure skate   patín
12. blade   cuchilla

E. Ice Skating Patinaje sobre Hielo
13. skater   patinador
14. skate   patín
15. ice   hielo

F. Bobsledding Bobsleigh
16. bobsled   bob
17. helmet   casco

G. Snowmobiling Motos de Nieve
18. snowmobile   moto de nieve

SPECTATOR SPORTS
DEPORTES PARA ESPECTADORES

15. home (plate)   home
16. umpire   árbitro
17. spectator   espectador
18. baseball   pelota de béisbol
19. batter   bateador
20. bat   bate
21. helmet   casco
22. uniform   uniforme
23. catcher   catcher
24. mask   protector
25. (baseball) glove/mitt guante (de béisbol)
26. shin guard   espinillera

B. Football Fútbol Americano

27. (football) field campo (de fútbol)
28. fullback/ runningback zaguero
29. halfback/ runningback medio
30. right end/ wide receiver extremo derecho
31. tight end   extremo derecho de cierre
32. right tackle placador derecho
33. right guard   apoyo derecho
34. center   central
35. quarterback   receptor
36. left guard   extremo izquierdo de cierre
37. left tackle   placador izquierdo
38. left end/ wide receiver extremo izquierdo
39. football balón de fútbol americano

A. Baseball Béisbol

1. stadium   estadio
2. stadium lights focos del estadio
3. foul line   línea de foul
4. (pitcher's) mound montículo del pitcher
5. pitcher   pitcher
6. first base   primera base
7. first baseman segunda base
8. outfielder   jardinero
9. second baseman segunda base (jugador)
10. second base segunda base
11. shortstop   shortstop
12. third baseman tercera base (jugador)
13. coach   entrenador
14. third base   tercera base

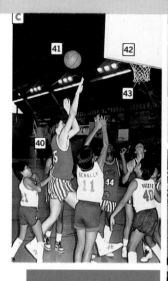

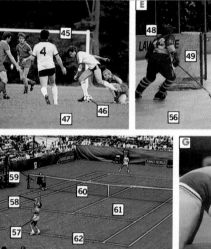

49. goal   portería
50. goalie   portero
51. mask   máscara
52. glove   guante
53. skate   patín
54. puck   disco
55. (hockey) stick
    bastón (de hockey)
56. ice   hielo

C. Basketball
Baloncesto

40. (basketball) player
    jugador (de baloncesto)
41. basketball
    pelota de baloncesto
42. backboard   tablero
43. basket   canasta

D. Soccer
Fútbol

44. (soccer) player
    futbolista
45. goal   portería
46. (soccer) ball
    balón (de fútbol)
47. (soccer) field
    campo (de fútbol)

E. Ice Hockey
Hockey sobre Hielo

48. (hockey) player
    jugador (de hockey)

F. Tennis
Tenis

57. (tennis) player
    tenista
58. (tennis) racket
    raqueta (de tenis)
59. (tennis) ball
    pelota (de tenis)
60. net   red
61. (tennis) court
    campo (de tenis)
62. baseline   línea de saque

G. Wrestling
Lucha Libre

63. wrestler   luchador
64. mat   lona

H. Karate
Karate

65. (black) belt
    cinturón (negro)

I. Boxing
Boxeo

66. boxer   boxeador
67. (boxing) glove
    guante (de boxeo)
68. trunks   pantalón
69. referee   árbitro
70. rope   cuerda
71. ring   ring

J. Horse Racing
Carreras de Caballos

72. gate   salida

A. Jogging
Footing

1. jogger
   practicante de footing

B. Running
Carrera

2. runner   corredor

C. Cycling
Ciclismo

3. cyclist   ciclista
4. helmet   casco/chichonera
5. bicycle/bike   bicicleta
6. (bicycle) pack
   cesta (de bicicleta)
7. wheel   rueda

D. Horseback
Riding
Equitación

8. (horseback) rider   jinete
9. horse   caballo
10. reins   riendas
11. saddle   silla de montar
12. stirrup   estribo

E. Archery   Arco

13. archer   arquero
14. bow   arco
15. arrow   flecha
16. target   blanco

F. Golf   Golf

17. golfer   golfista
18. (golf) club   palo (de golf)
19. (golf) ball   pelota (de golf)
20. hole   hoyo
21. green   green

G. Hiking
Excursionismo

22. hiker   excursionista
23. backpack   mochila
24. hiking boot   botas
25. trail   camino

H. Camping
Acampada

26. camper   campista
27. tent   tienda

I. Volleyball
Balonvolea

28. (volleyball) player
    jugador de balonvolea
29. volleyball   balonvolea
30. net   red

J. Rollerskating
Patinaje Sobre Ruedas

31. roller skater   patinador
32. roller skate   patín de ruedas
33. rink   pista

K. Bowling
Bolos/Boliche

34. bowler   lanzador
35. (bowling) ball   bola
36. gutter   carril
37. alley   calle
38. pin   bolo

L. Ping Pong/ Table Tennis
Ping Pong/Tenis de Mesa

39. (ping pong) player
    jugador (de ping pong)
40. paddle   raqueta
41. (ping pong) ball
    bola (de ping pong)
42. net   red
43. (ping pong) table
    mesa de (ping pong)

M. Handball
Pelota Vasca

44. (handball) player
    jugador (de frontón)
45. glove   guante

N. Squash
Squash

46. (squash) player
    jugador (de squash)
47. (squash) racket
    raqueta (de squash)
48. (squash) ball
    pelota (de squash)

O. Badminton
Bádminton

49. (badminton) player
    jugador (de bádminton)
50. (badminton) racket
    raqueta (de bádminton)
51. shuttlecock
    pelota de bádminton
52. Court   pista

A. Symphony
Concierto
1. orchestra   orquesta
2. podium   podio
3. conductor   director
4. (sheet) music   partitura
5. music stand   atril

B. Opera   Opera
6. chorus   coro
7. singer   cantante

C. Ballet   Ballet
8. ballerina   bailarina
9. ballet dancer   bailarín
10. toe shoe   zapatilla de ballet

D. Theater   Teatro
11. actress   actriz
12. actor   actor
13. stage   escenario
14. audience   público
15. aisle   pasillo
16. spotlight   foco
17. footlights   candilejas
18. orchestra pit   foso de orquesta

E. Movie Theater
Cine
19. marquee   marquesina
20. billboard   cartelera

F. Rock Concert
Concierto de Rock
21. singer/vocalist
    cantante/vocalista

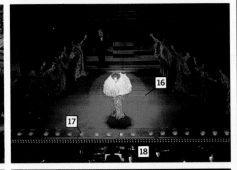

MUSICAL INSTRUMENTS
INSTRUMENTOS MUSICALES

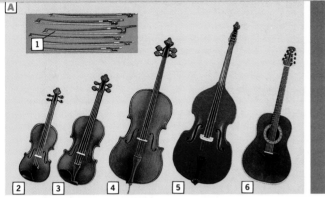

A. Strings
Cuerda

1. bow   arco
2. violin   violín
3. viola   viola
4. cello
   violonchelo | violoncelo
5. bass   contrabajo
6. guitar   guitarra

B. Brass
Metal

7. trombone   trombón
8. French horn
   cuerno francés
9. tuba   tuba
10. trumpet   trompeta

C. Woodwinds
Viento

11. flute   flauta (travesera)
12. recorder   flauta (dulce)
13. oboe   oboe
14. clarinet   clarinete
15. saxophone   saxofón
16. bassoon   fagot

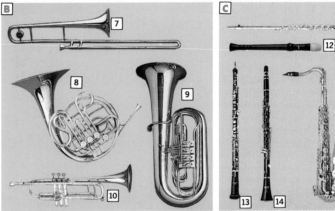

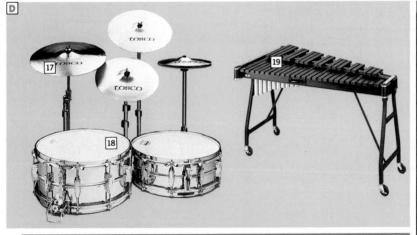

D. Percussion
Percusión

17. cymbal   platillo
18. drum   tambor
19. xylophone   xilófono

E. Other
Instruments
Otros Instrumentos

20. piano   piano
21. accordion   acordeón
22. harmonica   armónica

THE ZOO & PETS
EL ZOOLÓGICO Y LOS ANIMALES DOMÉSTICOS

A. The Zoo
El Zoo

1. lion   león
2. mane   melena
3. tiger   tigre
4. paw   pata
5. tail   cola
6. leopard   leopardo
7. spot   mancha

8. elephant   elefante
9. tusk   colmillo
10. trunk   trompa
11. rhinoceros   rinoceronte
12. horn   cuerno
13. hippopotamus   hipopótamo
14. bear   oso
15. polar bear   oso polar

16. buffalo   búfalo
17. zebra   cebra
18. stripe   raya
19. camel   camello
20. hump   joroba
21. giraffe   jirafa
22. deer   ciervo
23. antler   cuerno

24. llama   llama
25. koala bear   oso coala
26. kangaroo   canguro
27. pouch   marsupio
28. monkey   mono
29. gorilla   gorila
30. fox   zorro
31. raccoon   mapache

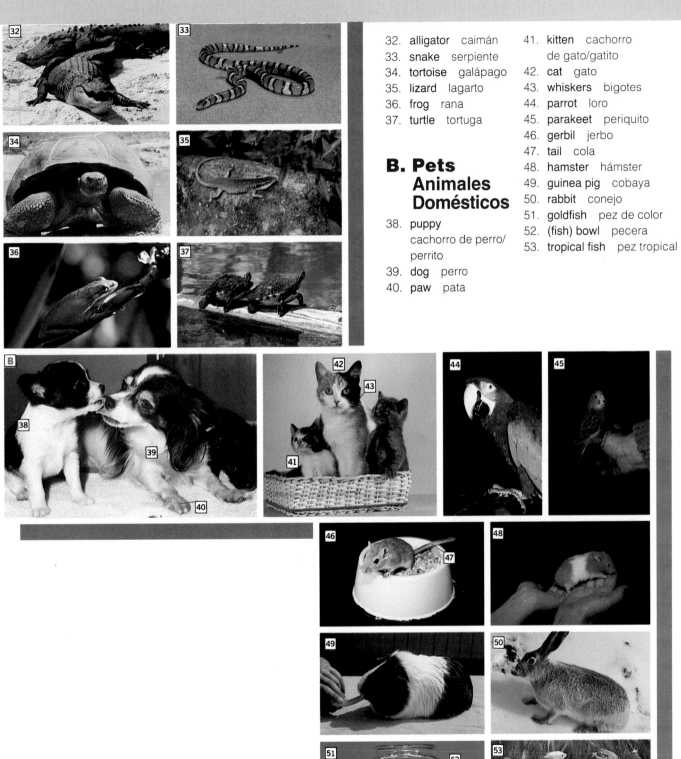

32. **alligator** caimán
33. **snake** serpiente
34. **tortoise** galápago
35. **lizard** lagarto
36. **frog** rana
37. **turtle** tortuga

B. Pets
Animales
Domésticos

38. **puppy**
     cachorro de perro/
     perrito
39. **dog** perro
40. **paw** pata

41. **kitten** cachorro
     de gato/gatito
42. **cat** gato
43. **whiskers** bigotes
44. **parrot** loro
45. **parakeet** periquito
46. **gerbil** jerbo
47. **tail** cola
48. **hamster** hámster
49. **guinea pig** cobaya
50. **rabbit** conejo
51. **goldfish** pez de color
52. **(fish) bowl** pecera
53. **tropical fish** pez tropical

THE FARM   LA GRANJA

1. **farmland** tierra de labor
2. **farmhouse** casa
3. **barn** granero
4. **silo** silo
5. **barnyard** corral
6. **fence** valla
7. **pond** estanque
8. **wheat field** trigal
9. **combine** cosechadora
10. **vegetable field** huerto
11. **farmer** granjero
12. **tractor** tractor
13. **furrow** surco
14. **crop** cultivo
15. **irrigation system** sistema de riego
16. **horse** caballo
17. **mane** crin
18. **pig** cerdo
19. **piglet** lechón
20. **pigpen/pig sty** pocilga
21. **cow** vaca
22. **calf** ternero
23. **bull** toro
24. **sheep** oveja
25. **lamb** cordero
26. **goat** cabra
27. **kid** chivo
28. **chicken/hen** gallina
29. **chick** polluelo/pollo
30. **rooster** gallo

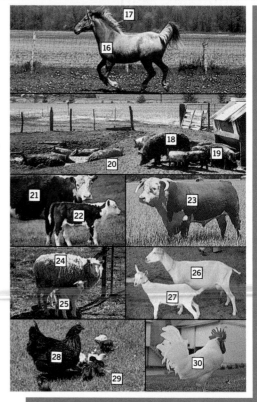

A. Fish
Peces

1. shark   tiburón
2. snout   hocico
3. fin   aleta
4. tail   cola
5. bass   róbalo
6. scale   escama
7. trout   trucha
8. gill   branquia
9. angelfish
   pez ángel
10. sunfish   peje-sol
11. eel   anguila

B. Sea Animals
Animales Marinos

12. octopus   pulpo
13. tentacle   tentáculo
14. whale   ballena
15. dolphin   delfín
16. seal   foca
17. flipper   aleta
18. walrus   morsa
19. tusk   colmillo
20. turtle   tortuga
21. lobster   langosta
22. shrimp   gamba
23. mussel   mejillón
24. crab   cangrejo
25. claw   pinza
26. clam   almeja
27. starfish   estrella
    de mar

BIRDS PÁJAROS

75

1. flamingo flamenco
2. pelican pelícano
3. bill pico
4. swan cisne
5. stork cigüeña
6. crane grulla
7. gull gaviota
8. duck pato
9. duckling patito
10. penguin pingüino
11. flipper ala
12. crow cuervo
13. ostrich avestruz
14. eagle águila
15. beak pico
16. hawk halcón
17. claw garra
18. owl búho
19. peacock pavo real
20. feather pluma
21. pigeon paloma
22. pheasant faisán
23. tail cola
24. robin petirrojo
25. blue jay arrendajo
26. hummingbird colibrí
27. wing ala
28. swallow golondrina
29. cockatoo cotorra
30. crest cresta
31. nest nido
32. egg huevo

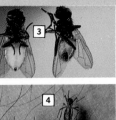

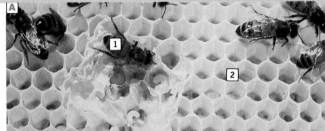

A. Insects
Insectos

1. **bee**   abeja
2. **honeycomb**   panal
3. **fly**   mosca
4. **mosquito**   mosquito
5. **cockroach/roach**   cucaracha
6. **caterpillar**   oruga
7. **butterfly**   mariposa
8. **ladybug**   mariquita
9. **cricket**   grillo
10. **ant**   hormiga
11. **dragonfly**   libélula
12. **spider***   araña[1]

B. Rodents
Roedores

13. **rat**   rata
14. **mouse**   ratón
15. **squirrel**   ardilla
16. **chipmunk**   ardilla listada

*not an insect

[1]no es un insecto

SPACE EL ESPACIO

1. **galaxy** galaxia
2. **star** estrella
3. **comet** cometa
4. **Sun** Sol
5. **planet/Saturn**
   planeta/Saturno

6. **Earth** la Tierra
7. **Moon** la Luna
8. **astronaut** astronauta
9. **space suit** traje
   espacial
10. **flag** bandera

11. **lunar module**
    módulo lunar
12. **lunar vehicle**
    vehículo lunar
13. **satelite** satélite
14. **space shuttle**
    transbordador espacial

15. **fuel tank**
    tanque de combustible
16. **booster rocket**
    cohete de propulsión

THE MILITARY · EL EJÉRCITO

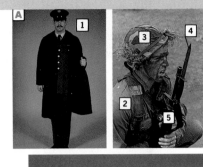

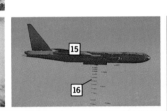

A. Army
Ejército de Tierra

1. soldier soldado
2. fatigues traje de faena
3. camouflage camuflaje
4. bayonet bayoneta
5. rifle fusil
6. machine gun ametralladora
7. jeep todo terreno/jeep
8. cannon cañón
9. tank tanque

B. Air Force
Fuerza Aérea

10. pilot piloto
11. parachute paracaídas
12. parachutist paracaidista
13. helicopter helicóptero
14. fighter plane cazabombardero
15. bomber bombardero
16. bomb bomba

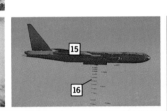

C. Navy
Marina

17. sailor marinero
18. submarine submarino
19. destroyer destructor
20. radar antenna antena de radar
21. battleship crucero
22. aircraft carrier portaaviones

D. Marines
Infantes de marina/Marines

A. Hobbies
Pasatiempos

1. coin collecting
   numismática
2. coin   moneda
3. (coin) album   álbum
   de monedas
4. coin catalog
   catálogo de monedas
5. magnifying glass
   lupa
6. stamp collecting
   filatelia
7. (stamp) album
   álbum de sellos
8. stamp   sello
9. stamp catalog
   catálogo de sellos
10. photography
    fotografía
11. camera   cámara
12. astronomy
    astronomía
13. telescope   telescopio
14. bird watching
    observación de aves

B. Crafts
Artesanía

15. sculpting   esculpir
16. sculpture   escultura
17. knitting   tricotar
18. knitting needle
    aguja de tricotar
19. weaving   tejer
20. loom   telar
21. pottery   cerámica
22. potter's wheel
    torno de cerámica
23. painting   pintar
24. brush   pincel
25. woodworking
    ebanistería

C. Games
Juegos

26. chess   ajedrez
27. board   tablero
28. checkers   damas
29. backgammon
    backgamon
30. Scrabble   Scrabble
31. Monopoly   Monopoly
32. cards   cartas

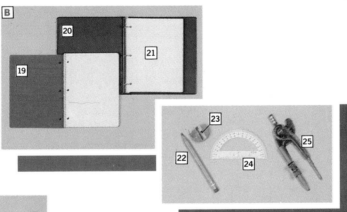

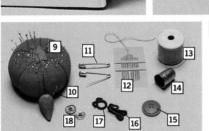

A. Sewing
Costura

1. sewing machine   máquina de coser
2. sewing basket   costurero
3. tape measure   cinta métrica
4. yarn   bobina de hilo
5. knitting needle   aguja de tricotar
6. (pair of) scissors   (par de) tijeras
7. zipper   cremallera
8. material   tela
9. pin cushion   acerico
10. straight pin   alfiler
11. safety pin   imperdible
12. needle   aguja
13. thread   carrete de hilo
14. thimble   dedal
15. button   botón
16. hook   corchete
17. eye   presilla
18. snap   broche a presión

B. Sundries
Artículos Diversos

19. (spiral) notebook   cuaderno (de espiral)
20. loose-leaf binder   cuaderno de anillas
21. (loose-leaf) paper   recambio
22. pencil   lápiz
23. pencil sharpener   sacapuntas
24. protractor   transportador
25. compass   compás
26. wrapping paper   papel de regalo
27. bow   lazo
28. box   caja
29. tissue paper   papel seda
30. ribbon   cinta
31. string   cuerda
32. masking tape   cinta adhesiva

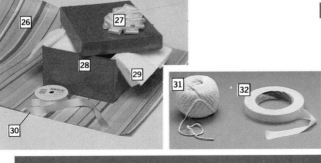

WORD LIST   LISTA DE PALABRAS

Esta lista de palabras es un índice alfabético de las entradas del *Diccionario Fotográfico Longman*. Los números en letra negra indican la página en que aparece la palabra; los demás números se refieren a los artículos de la página. Por ejemplo, "brush 25–3, 21; 50–15" significa que la palabra "brush" aparece en la página 25 en los ítems 3 y 21 asi como en la página 50 en el item 15.

accelerator /ək'sɛlə,reʸtər/ 55-22
accessories /ək'sɛsəriʸz/ 38-D
accordion /ə'kɔrdiʸən/ 70-21
action /'ækʃən/ 26; 27; 28
actor /'æktər/ 69-12
actress /'æktrɪs/ 69-11
acute angle /ə,kyuʷt 'æŋgəl/ 5-8
adapter /ə'dæptər/ 52-31
address /ə'drɛs, ædrɛs/ 19-16
adhesive tape /əd,hiʸsɪv 'teʸp/ 29-24
Afghanistan /æf'gænə,stæn/ 8
afraid /ə'freʸd/ 32-18
Africa /'æfrɪkə/ 8
after-shave /'æftər ʃeʸv/ 25-13
after-shave lotion /'æftər ʃeʸv ,loʷʃən/ 25-13
aircraft carrier /'ɛərkræft ,kæriʸər/ 78-22
air filter /'ɛər ,fɪltər/ 55-26
air force /'ɛər ,fɔrs/ 78-B
airport /'ɛərpɔrt/ 59; 60
air tank /'ɛər ,tæŋk/ 63-9
aisle /aɪl/ 69-15
aisle seat /'aɪl ,siʸt/ 60-33
Alabama /,ælə'bæmə/ 9
Alaska /ə'læskə/ 9
Albania /æl'beʸniʸə/ 8
Alberta /æl'bɜrtə/ 10
album /'ælbəm/ 79-3, 7
Algeria /æl'dʒiəriʸə/ 8
Alka Seltzer /'ælkə ,sɛltsər/ 29-20
alley /'æliʸ/ 68-37
alligator /'ælə,geʸtər/ 72-32
alternator /'ɔltər,neʸtər/ 55-29
aluminum foil /ə,luʷmənəm 'fɔɪl/ 45-30
A.M. /,eʸ 'em/ 2-i
amethyst /'æməθɪst/ 38-21
amplifier /'æmplə,faɪər/ 51-9
analog watch /,ænəlɔg 'watʃ/ 2-f
angelfish /'eʸndʒəl,fɪʃ/ 74-9
Angola /æŋ'goʷlə/ 8
angry /'æŋgriʸ/ 32-10
ankle /'æŋkəl/ 23-35
annoyed /ə'nɔɪd/ 32-12
answering machine /'ænsərɪŋ mə,ʃiʸn/ 51-21
ant /ænt/ 76-10
antacid /ænt,æsɪd/ 29-20
Antarctica /ænt'arktɪkə/ 7; 8
antenna /æn'tɛnə/ 39-15
antler /'æntlər/ 71-23
apartment building /ə'partmənt ,bɪldɪŋ/ 39-D
apex /'eʸpɛks/ 5-9

Appalachian Mountains /æpə,leʸtʃiʸən 'maʊntnz/ 9
appetizers /'æpə,taɪzərz/ 17-A
apple pie /'æpəl ,paɪ/ 17-19
apples /'æpəlz/ 151
apricots /'æprɪ,kats/ 15-12
April /'eʸprəl/ 3
Arabian Sea /ə,reʸbiʸən 'siʸ/ 8
archer /'artʃər/ 67-13
archery /'artʃəriʸ/ 67-E
architect /'arkə,tɛkt/ 22-36
Arctic Ocean /,arktɪk 'oʷʃən/ 7; 8
Argentina /,ardʒən'tiʸnə/ 7
Arizona /,ærə'zoʷnə/ 9
Arkansas /'arkənsɔ/ 9
arm /arm/ 23-11
armchair /'armtʃɛər/ 42-9
armrest /'armrɛst/ 60-37
army /'armiʸ/ 78-A
arrival and departure board /ə,raɪvəl ənd dɪ'partʃər ,bɔrd/ 56-4; 59-4
arrow /'æroʷ/ 67-15
artery /'artəriʸ/ 24-52
artichokes /'artə,tʃoʷks/ 16-20
artist /'artɪst/ 22-46
ashamed /ə'ʃeʸmd/ 32-15
Asia /'eʸʒə/ 8
asparagus /ə'spærəgəs/ 16-24
aspirin /'æspərɪn/ 29-10
astronaut /'æstrə,nɔt/ 79-12
astronomy /ə'stranəmiʸ/ 79-12
at night /ət 'naɪt/ 2-i
Atlantic Ocean /ət,læntɪk 'oʷʃən/ 7; 8; 9; 10
attaché case /ætə'ʃeʸ ,keʸs/ 38-27
attendant /ə'tɛndənt/ 55-5
audience /'ɔdiʸəns/ 69-14
audio cassette /,ɔdiʸoʷ kə'sɛt/ 51-20
August /'ɔgəst/ 3
aunt /ænt/ 31
Australia /ɔ'streʸliʸə/ 8
Austria /'ɔstriʸə/ 8
automatic teller /,ɔtəmætɪk 'tɛlər/ 6-8
avocados /,ævə'kadoʷz/ 15-7
awl /ɔl/ 40-24
azalea /ə'zeʸliʸə/ 40-21

baby /'beʸbiʸ/ 47-12
baby bottle /'beʸbiʸ ,batl/ 47-21
baby carrier /'beʸbiʸ ,kæriʸər/ 47-13
baby chair /'beʸbiʸ ,tʃɛər/ 47-9
baby clothes /'beʸbiʸ ,kloʷz/ 47-24
baby seat /'beʸbiʸ ,siʸt/ 47-18
back /bæk/ 23-26
backboard /'bækbɔrd/ 66-42
backgammon /'bæk,gæmən/ 79-29
backhoe /'bækhoʷ/ 53-12
backpack /'bækpæk/ 67-23
backyard /,bæk'yard/ 40
bacon /'beʸkən/ 14-20
bad /bæd/ 33-12
Baffin Bay /,bæfɪn 'beʸ/ 7; 10
Baffin Island /,bæfɪn 'aɪlənd/ 10
bag /bæg/ 13-7
baggage claim area /'bægɪdʒ kleʸm ,ɛriʸə/ 59-12
baggage claim check

/'bægɪdʒ kleʸm ,tʃɛk/ 59-17
Bahamas /bə'haməz/ 7
Bahrain /ba'reʸn/ 8
baked potato /,beʸkt pə'teʸtoʷ/ 17-7
baker /'beʸkər/ 21-20
baking potatoes /'beʸkɪŋ pə,teʸtoʷz/ 16-12
balcony /'bælkəniʸ/ 29-24
ball /bɔl/ 6214; 66-46, 59; 67-19; 68-35, 41, 48
ballerina /,bælə'riʸnə/ 69-8
ballet /'bæ'leʸ/ 69-C
ballet dancer /bæ'leʸ ,dænsər/ 69-9
ball point pen /,bɔl pɔɪnt 'pɛn/ 20-25
Baltic Sea /,bɔltɪk 'siʸ/ 8
bananas /bə'nænəz/ 15-8
bandage /'bændɪdʒ/ 29-25
Band-Aid /'bænd eʸd/ 29-22
Bangladesh /,bæŋglə'dɛʃ/ 8
bank book /'bæŋk bʊk/ 6-15
banking /'bæŋkɪŋ/ 6
bank officer /'bæŋk ,ɔfəsər/ 6-3
bank vault /'bæŋk ,vɔlt/ 6-6
bar /bar/ 47-3
barbecue /'barbɪkyuʷ/ 40-7
barber /'barbər/ 22-41
Barents Sea /,bɛrənts 'siʸ/ 8
barge /bardʒ/ 61-18
barn /barn/ 73-3
barnyard /'barnyard/ 73-5
barrette /bə'rɛt/ 38-5
base /beʸs/ 5-11; 25-1
baseball /'beʸsbɔl/ 65-A, 18
baseball glove /'beʸsbɔl ,glʌv/ 65-25
baseline /'beʸslaɪn/ 66-62
basket /'bæskɪt/ 66-13
basketball /'bæskɪt,bɔl/ 66-C, 41
basketball player /'bæskɪtbɔl ,pleʸər/ 66-40
bass /beʸs/ 70-5
bass /bæs/ 74-5
bassoon /bə'suʷn/ 70-16
bat /bæt/ 65-20
bathing suit /'beʸðɪŋ ,suʷt/ 62-17
bath mat /'bæθ ,mæt/ 44-7
bathroom /'bæθruʷm/ 39-27; 44
bath rug /'bæθ ,rʌg/ 44-7
bath towel /'bæθ ,taʊəl/ 44-6
bathtub /'bæθtʌb/ 44-5
batter /'bætər/ 65-19
battery /'bætəriʸ/ 52-32; 55-27
battleship /'bætl,ʃɪp/ 78-21
bayonet /'beʸənɪt/ 78-4
beach /biʸtʃ/ 62
beach ball /'biʸtʃ bɔl/ 62-14
beach blanket /'biʸtʃ ,blæŋkɪt/ 62-4
beach chair /'biʸtʃ ,tʃɛr/ 62-7
beach hat /'biʸtʃ ,hæt/ 62-15
beach towel /'biʸtʃ ,taʊəl/ 62-5
beach umbrella /'biʸtʃ ʌm,brɛlə/ 62-8
beak /biʸk/ 75-15
bear /bɛər/ 71-14
beard /biərd/ 24-49
beater /'biʸtər/ 46-23
Beaufort Sea /,boʷfərt 'siʸ/ 10
bed /bɛd/ 43-4
bedroom /'bɛdruʷm/ 39-31; 43
bedspread /'bɛdsprɛd/ 43-5
bee /biʸ/ 76-1
beige /beʸʒ/ 36-28

Belgium /'bɛldʒəm/ 8
Belize /bə'liʸz/ 7
below freezing /bɪ,loʷ 'friʸzɪŋ/ 4-f
below zero /bɪ,loʷ 'zɪəroʷ/ 4-g
belt /bɛlt/ 35-14; 66-65
belt buckle /'bɛlt ,bʌkəl/ 35-15
bench /bɛntʃ/ 48-6
bend /bɛnd/ 27-1
Benin /bɛ'niʸn/ 8
Bering Sea /,bɪərɪŋ 'siʸ/ 8
beverages /'bɛvərɪdʒɪz/ 17-E
Bhutan /buʷ'tan/ 8
bib /bɪb/ 47-19
bicycle /'baɪsɪkəl/ 67-5
bicycle pack /'baɪsɪkəl ,pæk/ 67-6
bike /baɪk/ 67-5
bike route sign /'baɪk ruʷt ,saɪn/ 58-39
bill /bɪl/ 75-3
billboard /'bɪlbɔrd/ 69-20
birds /bɜrdz/ 75
bird watching /'bɜrd ,watʃɪŋ/ 79-14
bit /bɪt/ 50-30
black /blæk/ 36-27
black belt /'blæk ,bɛlt/ 66-65
Black Sea /,blæk 'siʸ/ 8
blade /bleʸd/ 64-12
blanket /'blæŋkɪt/ 62-4
blasting mat /'blæstɪŋ ,mæt/ 53-13
blazer /'bleʸzər/ 36-8
blender /'blɛndər/ 46-17
blonde /bland/ 24-37
blood pressure gauge /'blʌd ,prɛʃər ,geʸdʒ/ 29-3
blouse /blaʊs, blaʊz/ 36-4
blue /bluʷ/ 35-27
blueberries /'bluʷ,bɛriʸz/ 1522
blue jay /'bluʷ ,dʒeʸ/ 75-25
blush /blʌʃ/ 25-2
board /bɔrd/ 79-27
boarding pass /'bɔrdɪŋ ,pæs/ 59-11
boardwalk /'bɔrdwɔk/ 62-2
bobsled /'babslɛd/ 64-16
bobsledding /'babslɛdɪŋ/ 64-F
body /'badiʸ/ 23
Bolivia /bə'lɪviʸə/ 7
bolt /boʷlt/ 50-7
bomb /bam/ 78-16
bomber /'bamər/ 78-15
book /bʊk/ 41-12
book of stamps /,bʊk əv 'stæmps/ 19-13
bookcase /'bʊk-keʸs/ 41-11
booster rocket /'buʷstər ,rakɪt/ 77-16
boot /buʷt/ 37-21; 64-4
bored /bɔrd/ 32-23
Botswana /bat'swanə/ 8
bottle /'batl/ 47-21
bottle opener /'batl ,oʷpənər/ 46-29
bow /baʊ/ 61-6
bow /boʷ/ 67-14; 70-1; 80-27
bowl /boʷl/ 42-15; 45-21; 46-9; 72-5
bowler /'boʷlər/ 68-34
bowling /'boʷlɪŋ/ 68-K
bowling ball /'boʷlɪŋ ,bɔl/ 68-35
box /baks/ 80-28
boxer /'baksər/ 66-66
boxer shorts /'baksər ,ʃɔrts/ 35-17

boxing /'bɑksɪŋ/ **66**-1
boxing glove /'bɑksɪŋ ˌglʌv/ **66**-67
box spring /'bɑks ˌsprɪŋ/ **43**-22
bra /brɑ/ **36**-16
brace /breʸs/ **50**-32
bracelet /'breʸslɪt/ **38**-3
braces /'breʸsɪz/ **30**-18
brain /breʸn/ **24**-51
brake /breʸk/ **55**-21
brass /bræs/ **70**-B
Brazil /brəˈzɪl/ **7**
bread /brɛd/ **14**-27
brick /brɪk/ **53**-17
bricklayer /'brɪkˌleʸər/ **21**-2
bridge /brɪdʒ/ **58**-D
briefcase /'briʸfkeʸs/ **38**-25
briefs /briʸfs/ **35**-18
British Columbia /ˌbrɪtɪʃ kəˈlʌmbiʸə/ **10**
broccoli /'brɑkəliʸ/ **16**-25; **17**-18
broken line /ˌbroʷkən ˈlaɪn/ **57**-3
brook /brʊk/ **54**-15
broom /bruʷm, brʊm/ **49**-7
brother /'brʌðər/ **31**
brother-in-law /'brʌðər ɪn ˌlɔ/ **31**
brothers /'brʌðərz/ **31**
brothers-in-law /'brʌðərz ɪn ˌlɔ/ **31**
brown /braʊn/ **35**-21
brunette /bruˈnɛt/ **24**-38
brush /brʌʃ/ **25**-3, 21; **50**-15; **79**-24
brush your hair /ˌbrʌʃ yər ˈhɛər/ **26**-11
brush your teeth /ˌbrʌʃ yər ˈtiʸθ/ **26**-5
bucket /'bʌkɪt/ **49**-13; **62**-18
buckle /'bʌkəl/ **35**-15
buffalo /'bʌfəloʷ/ **71**-16
buffet /bəˈfeʸ/ **42**-20
bulb /bʌlb/ **49**-28
Bulgaria /bʌlˈgɛəriʸə/ **8**
bull /bʊl/ **73**-23
bulletin board /'bʊlətn ˌbɔrd/ **20**-18
bumper /'bʌmpər/ **55**-10
buoy /'buʷiʸ/ **61**-17
Burma /'bɜrmə/ **8**
burner /'bɜrnər/ **45**-14
Burundi /bʊˈrʊndiʸ/ **8**
bus /bʌs/ **12**-25; **56**-11; **57**-12
bush /bʊʃ/ **40**-12
bus lane /'bʌs ˌleʸn/ **11**-12
bus station /'bʌs ˌsteʸʃən/ **56**-B
bus stop /'bʌs ˌstɑp/ **12**-23
butcher /'bʊtʃər/ **21**-19
butter /'bʌtər/ **13**-16
butterfly /'bʌtərˌflaɪ/ **76**-7
buttocks /'bʌtəks/ **23**-32
button /'bʌtn/ **80**-15

cabbage /'kæbɪdʒ/ **16**-29
cabin /'kæbɪn/ **60**-26
cabinet /'kæbənɪt/ **45**-24
cake pan /'keʸk ˌpæn/ **46**-8
cake stand /'keʸk ˌstænd/ **45**-8
calculator /'kælkyəˌleʸtər/ **52**-29
calendar /'kæləndər/ **3**
calf /kæf/ **23**-34; **73**-22
California /ˌkæləˈfɔrnyə/ **9**
camel /'kæməl/ **71**-19

camera /'kæmərə/ **52**-39; **79**-11
Cameroon /ˌkæməˈruʷn/ **8**
camouflage /'kæməˌflɑʒ/ **78**-3
camper /'kæmpər/ **67**-26
camping /'kæmpɪŋ/ **67**-H
can /kæn/ **50**-19
Canada /'kænədə/ **7**; **10**
candy bar /'kændiʸ ˌbar/ **18**-16
canister /'kænəstər/ **45**-4
canned goods /'kænd ˌgʊdz/ **14**-D
cannon /'kænən/ **78**-8
canoe /kəˈnuʷ/ **63**-29
canoeing /kəˈnuʷɪŋ/ **63**-K
canoeist /kəˈnuʷɪst/ **63**-28
can opener /'kæn ˌoʷpənər/ **46**-16
cantaloupes /'kæntəlˌoʷps/ **15**-25
cap /kæp/ **37**-3; **47**-22
captain /'kæptən/ **60**-23
car /kar/ **55**; **57**-11
cardigan /'kardəgən/ **37**-12
cards /kardz/ **79**-32
cargo /'kargoʷ/ **61**-9
cargo ship /'kargoʷ ˌʃɪp/ **61**-8
Caribbean Sea /ˌkærəbiʸən ˈsiʸ/ **7**
carousel /ˌkærəˈsɛl/ **59**-16
carpenter /'karpəntər/ **21**-3
carpet /'karpɪt/ **43**-7
carpet sweeper /'karpɪt ˌswiʸpər/ **49**-8
carriage /'kærɪdʒ/ **47**-14
carrots /'kærəts/ **16**-23
carry /'kæriʸ/ **28**-7
carry-on-bag /'kæriʸ an ˌbæg/ **60**-28
carry-on-luggage /'kæriʸ an ˌlʌgɪdʒ/ **60**-28
car seat /'kar ˌsiʸt/ **47**-15
cashier /kæ ˈʃɪər/ **13**-2
cash machine /'kæʃ məˌʃiʸn/ **6**-8
cash register /'kæʃ ˌrɛdʒəstər/ **13**-3
Caspian Sea /ˌkæspiʸən ˈsiʸ/ **8**
casserole /'kæsəˌroʷl/ **46**-4
cassette /kəˈsɛt/ **51**-2, 20
cassette deck /kəˈsɛt ˌdɛk/ **51**-11
cassette player /kəˈsɛt ˌpleʸər/ **51**-17
casual wear /'kæʒuʷəl ˌwɛər/ **35**-B; **36**-B
cat /kæt/ **72**-42
catch /kætʃ/ **27**-11
catcher /'kætʃər/ **65**-23
caterpillar /'kætərˌpɪlər/ **76**-6
cauliflower /'kɔliˌflaʊər/ **16**-17
CD /ˌsiʸ ˈdiʸ/ **51**-14
ceiling /'siʸlɪŋ/ **41**-28
celery /'sɛləriʸ/ **16**-7
cello /'tʃɛloʷ/ **70**-4
cement /sɪˈmɛnt/ **53**-15
cement mixer /sɪˈmɛnt ˌmɪksər/ **53**-14
center /'sɛntər/ **5**-18; **65**-34
centerpiece /'sɛntərˌpiʸs/ **42**-1
centimeters /'sɛntəˌmiʸtərz/ **5**-28
Central African Republic /ˌsɛntrəl ˈæfrɪkən rɪˈpʌblɪk/ **8**
cereal /'sɪəriʸəl/ **14**-28
certified mail /ˌsɜrtəfaɪd ˈmeʸl/ **19**-21

Chad /tʃæd/ **8**
chain /tʃeʸn/ **38**-1
chair /tʃɛər/ **40**-11; **42**-8; **62**-7
chair lift /'tʃɛər ˌlɪft/ **64**-6
chandelier /ˌʃændəˈlɪər/ **42**-22
change lane /'tʃeʸndʒ ˌleʸn/ **57**-16
change purse /'tʃeʸndʒ ˌpɜrs/ **38**-28
changing pad /'tʃeʸndʒɪŋ ˌpæd/ **47**-1
check /tʃɛk/ **6**-11
checkbook /'tʃɛkbʊk/ **6**-9; **13**-4
checked /tʃɛkt/ **35**-28
checkers /'tʃɛkərz/ **79**-28
check-in-counter /'tʃɛk ɪn ˌkaʊntər/ **59**-8
check-out area /'tʃɛk aʊt ˌɛəriʸə/ **13**-A
check-out counter /'tʃɛk aʊt ˌkaʊntər/ **13**-8
check register /'tʃɛk ˌrɛdʒəstər/ **6**-10
cheek /tʃiʸk/ **24**-46
cheese /tʃiʸz/ **13**-13
chef /ʃɛf/ **21**-21
cherries /'tʃɛriʸz/ **15**-11
chess /tʃɛs/ **79**-26
chest /tʃɛst/ **23**-9; **43**-9; **47**-5
chest of drawers /ˌtʃɛst əv ˈdrɔrz/ **43**-9; **47**-5
chewing gum /'tʃuʷɪŋ ˌgʌm/ **18**-17
chick /tʃɪk/ **73**-29
chicken /'tʃɪkən/ **14**-23; **73**-28
child /tʃaɪld/ **47**-2; **48**-3
children /'tʃɪldrən/ **31**
Chile /'tʃɪliʸ/ **7**
chilly /'tʃɪliʸ/ **4**-c
chimney /'tʃɪmniʸ/ **39**-6
chin /tʃɪn/ **23**-8
China /'tʃaɪnə/ **8**
chipmunk /'tʃɪpmʌŋk/ **76**-16
chisel /'tʃɪzəl/ **50**-25
chocolate /'tʃɔkəlɪt/ **18**-16
chocolate cake /'tʃɔkəlɪt ˌkeʸk/ **17**-20
chorus /'kɔrəs/ **69**-6
Christmas /'krɪsməs/ **3**-13
circle /'sɜrkəl/ **5**-F
circumference /sərˈkʌmfərəns/ **5**-17
city /'sɪtiʸ/ **11**
claim check /'kleʸm ˌtʃɛk/ **59**-17
clam /klæm/ **74**-26
clarinet /ˌklærəˈnɛt/ **70**-14
claw /klɔ/ **74**-25; **75**-17
clean /kliʸn/ **33**-17
clear /klɪər/ **4**-9
cliff /klɪf/ **54**-9
clock /klɑk/ **2**-a; **56**-2
clock radio /ˌklɑk ˈreʸdiʸˌoʷ/ **51**-16
closed /kloʷzd/ **34**-30
closet /'klɑzɪt/ **39**-29
clothes /kloʷz/ **47**-24
clothesline /'kloʷzˌlaɪn/ **49**-24
clothespin /'kloʷzˌpɪn/ **49**-23
cloudy /'klaʊdiʸ/ **4**-10
club /klʌb/ **67**-18
club chair /'klʌb ˌtʃɛər/ **41**-4
clutch /klʌtʃ/ **55**-20
clutch bag /'klʌtʃ ˌbæg/ **36**-7
coach /koʷtʃ/ **65**-13
coat /koʷt/ **37**-1

cockatoo /'kɑkəˌtuʷ/ **75**-29
cockpit /'kɑkˌpɪt/ **60**-22
cockroach /'kɑk-roʷtʃ/ **76**-5
coconuts /'koʷkəˌnʌts/ **15**-6
coffee /'kɔfiʸ/ **17**-23
coffee maker /'kɔfiʸ ˌmeʸkər/ **46**-14
coffee pot /'kɔfiʸ ˌpat/ **45**-16
coffee table /'kɔfi ˌteʸbəl/ **41**-6
coin /kɔɪn/ **79**-2
coin album /'kɔɪn ˌælbəm/ **79**-3
coin catalog /'kɔɪn ˌkætl-ɔg/ **79**-4
coin collecting /'kɔɪn kəˌlɛktɪŋ/ **79**-1
cold /koʷld/ **4**-d; **29**-13; **34**-28
cold tablets /'koʷld ˌtæblɪts/ **29**-15
cold water faucet /ˌkoʷld ˈwɔtər ˌfɔsɪt/ **44**-23
collar /'kɑlər/ **35**-6
collar bar /'kɑlər ˌboʷn/ **38**-13
cologne /kəˈloʷn/ **25**-16
Colombia /kəˈlʌmbiʸə/ **7**
Colorado /ˌkɑləˈrædoʷ/ **9**
colors /'kʌlərz/ **35**-D; **36**-D
comb /koʷm/ **25**-15
comb your hair /ˌkoʷm yər ˈhɛər/ **26**-20
combine /'kɑmbaɪn/ **73**-9
comet /'kɑmɪt/ **77**-3
comforter /'kʌmfərtər/ **43**-18
compact disc /ˌkɑmpækt ˈdɪsk/ **51**-14
compact disc player /ˌkɑmpækt ˈdɪsk ˌpleʸər/ **51**-13
compass /'kʌmpəs/ **80**-25
computer /kəmˈpyuʷtər/ **6**-5; **52**-23
computer technician /kəmˈpyuʷtər tɛkˌnɪʃən/ **22**-34
conductor /kənˈdʌktər/ **69**-3
confused /kənˈfyuʷzd/ **32**-24
Congo /'kɑŋgoʷ/ **8**
Connecticut /kəˈnɛtɪkət/ **9**
construction /kənˈstrʌkʃən/ **53**
construction worker /kənˈstrʌkʃən ˌwɜrkər/ **21**-1; **53**-1
control /kənˈtroʷl/ **43**-20
control tower /kənˈtroʷl ˌtaʊər/ **60**-44
convertible /kənˈvɜrtəbəl/ **55**-36
cook /kʊk/ **21**-21; **25**-12
cookbook /'kʊk-bʊk/ **45**-9
cookies /'kʊkiʸz/ **14**-29
cookie sheet /'kʊkiʸ ˌʃiʸt/ **46**-10
cool /kuʷl/ **4**-c
cool air duct /ˌkuʷl ˈɛər dʌkt/ **55**-30
coolant recovery tank /ˌkuʷlənt rɪˈkʌvəriʸ ˌtæŋk/ **55**-31
co-pilot /'koʷˌpaɪlət/ **60**-24
copper pot /ˌkɑpər ˈpat/ **45**-15
Coral Sea /ˌkɔrəl ˈsiʸ/ **8**
corn /kɔrn/ **16**-26
corner /'kɔrnər/ **5**-1; **11**-13; **58**-23
corridor /'kɔrədər/ **39**-25
cosmetics /kɑzˈmɛtɪks/ **25**-A
Costa Rica /ˌkoʷstə ˈriʸkə/ **7**
couch /kaʊtʃ/ **41**-1
cough /kɔf/ **29**-16
cough drops /'kɔf drɑps/ **29**-18
cough syrup /'kɔf ˌsɪrəp/ **29**-17
counter /'kaʊntər/ **6**-4; **45**-20
court /kɔrt/ **66**-61; **68**-52

cousins /ˈkʌzənz/ **31**
cover /ˈkʌvər/ **46**-2
cow /kaʊ/ **73**-21
crab /kræb/ **74**-24
crackers /ˈkrækərz/ **14**-30
crafts /kræfts/ **79**-B
crane /kreʸn/ **53**-8; **61**-15; **75**-6
creamer /ˈkriʸmər/ **45**-17
credit card /ˈkrɛdɪt ˌkɑrd/ **6**-17
crest /krɛst/ **75**-30
crewneck /ˈkruʷnɛk/ **37**-9
crib /krɪb/ **47**-4
cricket /ˈkrɪkɪt/ **76**-9
crooked /ˈkrʊkɪd/ **34**-38
crop /krɑp/ **73**-14
cross country skiing
/ˌkrɔs kʌntriʸ ˈskiʸɪŋ/ **64**-C
crosswalk /ˈkrɔswɔk/ **11**-10; **58**-21
crow /kroʷ/ **75**-12
Cuba /ˈkyuʷbə/ **7**
cube /kyuʷb/ **5**-A
cucumbers /ˈkyuʷkʌmbərz/ **16**-6
cuff link /ˈkʌf ˌlɪŋk/ **38**-14
cup /kʌp/ **42**-17; **44**-16; **45**-18
cupboard /ˈkʌbərd/ **45**-24
curb /kɜrb/ **11**-14
curly /ˈkɜrliʸ/ **33**-24
curve sign /ˈkɜrv ˌsaɪn/ **58**-19
cushion /ˈkʊʃən/ **41**-2
customer /ˈkʌstəmər/ **6**-2; **13**-1
customs /ˈkʌstəmz/ **59**-18
customs officer
/ˈkʌstəmz ˌɔfəsər/ **59**-19
cut /kʌt/ **28**-12; **29**-21
cutting board /ˈkʌtɪŋ ˌbɔrd/ **45**-26
cycling /ˈsaɪklɪŋ/ **67**-C
cyclist /ˈsaɪklɪst/ **67**-3
cylinder /ˈsɪləndər/ **5**-H
cymbal /ˈsɪmbəl/ **70**-17
Cyprus /ˈsaɪprəs/ **8**
Czechoslovakia
/ˌtʃɛkəsloʷˈvɑkiʸə/ **8**

daffodil /ˈdæfəˌdɪl/ **40**-26
dairy /ˈdeəriʸ/ **13**-C
daisy /ˈdeʸziʸ/ **40**-20
dark /dɑrk/ **34**-36
dashboard /ˈdæʃbɔrd/ **55**-13
daughter /ˈdɔtər/ **31**
daughter-in-law /ˈdɔtər ɪn ˌlɔ/ **31**
days of the week
/ˌdeʸz əv ðə ˈwiʸk/ **3**-C
December /dɪˈsɛmbər/ **3**
deck /dɛk/ **61**-10
deer /dɪər/ **71**-22
degrees Celsius
/dɪˌgriʸz ˈsɛlsiʸəs/ **4**-15
degrees Centigrade
/dɪˌgriʸz ˈsɛntəgreʸd/ **4**-15
degrees Fahrenheit
/dɪˌgriʸz ˈfærənhaɪt/ **4**-14
Delaware /ˈdɛləwɛər/ **9**
Denmark /ˈdɛnmɑrk/ **8**
dental assistant
/ˈdɛntəl əˌsɪstənt/ **30**-4
dental floss /ˈdɛntəl ˌflɔs/ **30**-13
dental hygienist
/ˌdɛntəl haɪˈdʒiʸnɪst/ **22**-28
dentist /ˈdɛntɪst/ **22**-27; **30**-1
deposit slip /dɪˈpɑzɪt ˌslɪp/ **6**-13
depth /dɛpθ/ **5**-5

derrick /ˈdɛrɪk/ **61**-13
desert /ˈdɛzərt/ **54**-17
desk /dɛsk/ **20**-24
desk calendar
/ˈdɛsk ˌkæləndər/ **20**-23
desk lamp /ˈdɛsk ˌlæmp/ **20**-2
desserts /dɪˈzɜrts/ **17**-D
destroyer /dɪˈstrɔɪər/ **78**-19
detergent /dɪˈtɜrdʒənt/ **49**-17
determined /dɪˈtɜrmɪnd/ **32**-19
diagonal /daɪˈægənəl/ **5**-16
diameter /daɪˈæmətər/ **5**-19
diamond /ˈdaɪəmənd/ **38**-20
diaper /ˈdaɪəpər/ **47**-25
digital watch /ˌdɪdʒətl ˈwɑtʃ/ **2**-e
dill /dɪl/ **16**-32
dime /daɪm/ **6**-21
dining room /ˈdaɪnɪŋ ˌruʷm/ **39**-28; **42**
dining room table
/ˌdaɪnɪŋ ruʷm ˈteʸbəl/ **42**-7
dinner fork /ˈdɪnər ˌfɔrk/ **42**-11
dinner roll /ˈdɪnər ˌroʷl/ **17**-8
dirt road /ˈdɜrt ˌroʷd/ **58**-18
dirty /ˈdɜrtiʸ/ **33**-18
disc camera /ˈdɪsk ˌkæmərə/ **52**-37
disc film /ˈdɪsk ˌfɪlm/ **52**-38
disgusted /dɪsˈgʌstɪd/ **32**-13
dish towel /ˈdɪʃ ˌtaʊəl/ **45**-28
dishwasher /ˈdɪʃˌwɑʃər/ **45**-12
diskette /dɪˈskɛt/ **52**-25
display screen
/dɪˈspleʸ ˌskriʸn/ **52**-24
displeased /dɪsˈpliʸzd/ **32**-9
diver /ˈdaɪvər/ **63**-3
divided by /dɪˈvaɪdɪd baɪ/ **1**
divider /dɪˈvaɪdər/ **57**-6
diving /ˈdaɪvɪŋ/ **63**-B
diving board /ˈdaɪvɪŋ ˌbɔrd/ **63**-4
Djibouti /dʒɪˈbuʷtiʸ/ **8**
dock /dɑk/ **61**-2
dock worker /ˈdɑk ˌwɜrkər/ **61**-14
doctor /ˈdɑktər/ **22**-25; **29**-8
doctor's office /ˈdɑktərz ˌɔfɪs/ **29**-A
documents /ˈdɑkyəmənts/ **59**-20
dog /dɔg/ **72**-39
doll /dɑl/ **48**-15
dollar /ˈdɑlər/ **6**-25
dollar bill /ˌdɑlər ˈbɪl/ **6**-25
doll carriage /ˈdɑl ˌkærɪdʒ/ **48**-16
dolphin /ˈdɑlfɪn/ **74**-15
Dominican Republic
/dəˌmɪnɪkən rɪˈpʌblɪk/ **7**
do not enter sign
/duʷ nɑt ˈɛntər ˌsaɪn/ **58**-29
donut /ˈdoʷnʌt/ **18**-18
door /dɔr/ **56**-19
door handle /ˈdɔr ˌhændl/ **45**-25; **56**-18
doorknob /ˈdɔrnɑb/ **39**-13; **44**-12
double boiler /ˌdʌbəl ˈbɔɪlər/ **46**-1
double yellow lines
/ˌdʌbəl yeloʷ ˈlaɪnz/ **58**-20
downhill skiing
/ˌdaʊnhɪl ˈskiʸɪŋ/ **64**-B
downstairs apartment
/ˌdaʊnstɛərz əˈpɑrtmənt/ **39**-17

dragonfly /ˈdrægənˌflaɪ/ **76**-11
drape /dreʸp/ **41**-14
draw /drɔ/ **28**-13
drawer /drɔr/ **43**-10; **45**-23
dress /drɛs/ **36**-A, 6
dresser /ˈdrɛsər/ **43**-13
drill /drɪl/ **30**-3
drink /drɪŋk/ **26**-14
driver /ˈdraɪvər/ **56**-12
driveway /ˈdraɪvweʸ/ **39**-1
drum /drʌm/ **70**-18
dry /draɪ/ **33**-22
dry off /ˌdraɪ ˈɔf/ **26**-4
dryer /ˈdraɪər/ **49**-16
duck /dʌk/ **75**-8
duckling /ˈdʌklɪŋ/ **75**-9
dump truck /ˈdʌmp ˌtrʌk/ **53**-10
dune /duʷn/ **54**-18
duplex /ˈduʷplɛks/ **39**-C
dust /dʌst/ **26**-16
dust cloth /ˈdʌst klɔθ/ **49**-4
dust mop /ˈdʌst ˌmɑp/ **49**-11
dustpan /ˈdʌstpæn/ **49**-5
dust ruffle /ˈdʌst ˌrʌfəl/ **43**-6

eagle /ˈiʸgəl/ **75**-14
ear /ɪər/ **23**-4
earring /ˈɪərɪŋ/ **38**-6
Earth /ɜrθ/ **77**-6
east /iʸst/ **9**
East /iʸst/ **9**
East China Sea
/ˌiʸst tʃaɪnə ˈsiʸ/ **8**
Easter /ˈiʸstər/ **3**-5
East Germany
/ˌiʸst ˈdʒɜrməniʸ/ **8**
eat /iʸt/ **26**-13
ecstatic /ɪkˈstætɪk/ **32**-3
Ecuador /ˈɛkwəˌdɔr/ **7**
edge /ɛdʒ/ **5**-4
eel /iʸl/ **74**-11
egg /ɛg/ **75**-32
egg beater /ˈɛg ˌbiʸtər/ **46**-23
eggplants /ˈɛgplænts/ **16**-22
eggs /ɛgz/ **13**-14
Egypt /ˈiʸdʒɪpt/ **8**
El Salvador /ˌɛl ˈsælvədɔr/ **7**
elbow /ˈɛlboʷ/ **23**-29
electric blanket
/ɪˌlɛktrɪk ˈblæŋkɪt/ **43**-19
electric drill /ɪˌlɛktrɪk ˈdrɪl/ **50**-29
electrician /ɪˌlɛkˈtrɪʃən/ **21**-10
electric mixer
/ɪˌlɛktrɪk ˈmɪksər/ **46**-20
electric pencil sharpener
/ɪˌlɛktrɪk ˈpɛnsəl ˌʃɑrpənər/ **20**-5
electric shaver
/ɪˌlɛktrɪk ˈʃeʸvər/ **25**-23
electric typewriter
/ɪˌlɛktrɪk ˈtaɪpˌraɪtər/ **52**-36
electronics /ɪˌlɛkˈtrɑnɪks/ **51**; **52**
electronic typewriter
/ɪlɛkˌtrɑnɪk ˈtaɪpˌraɪtər/ **52**-35
elephant /ˈɛləfənt/ **71**-8
elevator /ˈɛləˌveʸtər/ **39**-21
ellipse /ɪˈlɪps/ **5**-G
embarrassed /ɪmˈbærəst/ **32**-14
emerald /ˈɛmərəld/ **38**-24
emery board /ˈɛməriʸ ˌbɔrd/ **25**-19

emotions /ɪˈmoʷʃənz/ **32**
empty /ˈɛmptiʸ/ **34**-32
end table /ˈɛnd ˌteʸbəl/ **41**-7
engine /ˈɛndʒən/ **55**-28
entertainment
/ˌɛntərˈteʸnmənt/ **69**
entrées /ˈɑntreʸz/ **17**-C
envelope /ˈɛnvəˌloʷp/ **19**-14
equals /ˈiʸkwəlz/ **1**
erase /ɪˈreʸs/ **28**-3
eraser /ɪˈreʸsər/ **20**-27
Ethiopia /iʸˈθiʸˈoʷpiʸə/ **8**
Europe /ˈyʊərəp/ **8**
exact change lane
/ɪgˌzækt ˈtʃeʸndʒ ˌleʸn/ **57**-15
examination table
/ɪgˌzæməˈneʸʃən ˌteʸbəl/ **29**-7
excavation site
/ˌɛkskəˈveʸʃən ˌsaɪt/ **53**-9
exit /ˈɛgzɪt/ **12**-26
express mail /ɪkˌsprɛs ˈmeʸl/ **19**-4
extension cord
/ɪkˈstɛnʃən ˌkɔrd/ **49**-29
eye /aɪ/ **23**-3; **80**-17
eyebrow /ˈaɪbraʊ/ **24**-42
eyebrow pencil
/ˈaɪbraʊ ˌpɛnsəl/ **25**-4
eyelash /ˈaɪlæʃ/ **24**-44
eyelid /ˈaɪlɪd/ **24**-43
eyeliner /ˈaɪˌlaɪnər/ **25**-5
eye shadow /ˈaɪ ˌʃædoʷ/ **25**-7

face /feʸs/ **2**-d; **23**-1
Falkland Islands
/ˈfɔklənd ˌaɪləndz/ **7**
fall /fɔl/ **4**-2; **28**-23
family /ˈfæməliʸ/ **31**
farm /fɑrm/ **73**
farmer /ˈfɑrmər/ **21**-16; **73**-11
farmhouse /ˈfɑrmhaʊs/ **73**-2
farmland /ˈfɑrmlænd/ **73**-1
fast /fæst/ **34**-25
fast foods /ˌfæst ˈfuʷdz/ **18**
father /ˈfɑðər/ **31**
father-in-law /ˈfɑðər ɪn ˌlɔ/ **31**
Father's Day /ˈfɑðərz ˌdeʸ/ **3**-8
fatigues /fəˈtiʸgz/ **78**-2
fatty tissue /ˈfætiʸ ˌtɪʃuʷ/ **24**-61
faucet /ˈfɔsɪt/ **45**-7
feather /ˈfɛðər/ **75**-20
February /ˈfɛbruʷˌɛriʸ/ **3**
fence /fɛns/ **73**-6
ferry /ˈfɛriʸ/ **61**-20
fever /ˈfiʸvər/ **29**-11
field /fiʸld/ **54**-8; **65**-27; **66**-47
fifty cent piece
/ˌfɪftiʸ sɛnt ˈpiʸs/ **6**-23
fighter plane /ˈfaɪtər ˌpleʸn/ **78**-14
figure skate /ˈfɪgyər ˌskeʸt/ **64**-11
figure skater /ˈfɪgyər ˌskeʸtər/ **64**-10
figure skating
/ˈfɪgyər ˌskeʸtɪŋ/ **64**-D
file cabinet /ˈfaɪl ˌkæbənɪt/ **20**-16
file folder /ˈfaɪl ˌfoʷldər/ **20**-1
filling /ˈfɪlɪŋ/ **30**-7
film /fɪlm/ **52**-42
fin /fɪn/ **74**-3
finger /ˈfɪŋgər/ **23**-15
Finland /ˈfɪnlənd/ **8**
firefighter /ˈfaɪərˌfaɪtər/ **21**-12

fire hydrant /ˈfaɪər ˌhaɪdrənt/ 11-3
fireplace /ˈfaɪərpleʸs/ 41-19
fireplace screen /ˈfaɪərpleʸs ˌskriʸn/ 41-20
first /fɜrst/ 1
first base /ˌfɜrst ˈbeʸs/ 65-6
first baseman /ˌfɜrst ˈbeʸsmæn/ 65-7
first floor /ˌfɜrst ˈflɔr/ 39-22
fish /fɪʃ/ 17-17; 74-A
fish bowl /ˈfɪʃ ˌboʷl/ 72-52
fisherman /ˈfɪʃərmən/ 21-15; 63-11
fishing /ˈfɪʃɪŋ/ 63-E
fishing line /ˈfɪʃɪŋ ˌlaɪn/ 63-13
fishing rod /ˈfɪʃɪŋ ˌrad/ 63-12
fitted sheet /ˌfɪtɪd ˈʃiʸt/ 43-16
flag /flæg/ 11-8; 77-10
flamingo /fləˈmɪŋgoʷ/ 75-1
flash /flæʃ/ 52-41
flat sheet /ˌflæt ˈʃiʸt/ 43-17
flight attendant /ˈflaɪt əˌtendənt/ 60-34
flipper /ˈflɪpər/ 74-17; 75-11
floor /flɔr/ 41-27
floor plan /ˈflɔr ˌplæn/ 39-E
floppy disc /ˌflapiʸ ˈdɪsk/ 52-25
Florida /ˈflɔrɪdə/ 9
florist /ˈflɔrɪst/ 21-17
flower bed /ˈflaʊər ˌbed/ 40-13
flowered /ˈflaʊərd/ 36-30
flowers /ˈflaʊərz/ 41-17
flute /fluʷt/ 70-11
fly /flaɪ/ 76-3
foggy /ˈfagiʸ/ 4-12
folding rule /ˌfoʷldɪŋ ˈruʷl/ 50-14
food processor /ˈfuʷd ˌprasesər 46-18
food warmer /ˈfuʷd ˌwɔrmər/ 47-23
foot /fʊt/ 5-27; 23-22
football /ˈfʊtbɔl/ 65-B, 39
football field /ˈfʊtbɔl ˌfiʸld/ 65-27
footlights /ˈfʊtlaɪts/ 69-17
footwear /ˈfʊt-weər/ 37-D
forearm /ˈfɔrarm/ 23-12
forehead /ˈfɔrhed/ 24-40
forest /ˈfɔrɪst/ 54-11
fork /fɔrk/ 42-10, 11
foul line /ˈfaʊl ˌlaɪn/ 65-3
foundation /faʊnˈdeʸʃən/ 25-1
fourth /fɔrθ/ 1
Fourth of July /ˌfɔrθ əv dʒʊˈlaɪ/ 3-9
fox /faks/ 71-30
frame /freʸm/ 41-23
France /fræns/ 8
freezer /ˈfriʸzər/ 45-10
freezing /ˈfriʸzɪŋ/ 4-e
freighter /ˈfreʸtər/ 61-8
french fries /ˌfrentʃ ˈfraɪz/ 18-27
French Guiana /ˌfrentʃ giʸˈænə/ 7
French horn /ˌfrentʃ ˈhɔrn/ 70-8
Friday /ˈfraɪdiʸ/ 3
fried chicken /ˌfraɪd ˈtʃɪkən/ 18-5
fried clams /ˌfraɪd ˈklæmz/ 18-4
frog /frɔg/ 72-36
front /frʌnt/ 5-3
front door /ˌfrʌnt ˈdɔr/ 39-14
frontend loader /ˌfrʌntend ˈloʷdər/ 53-11
front steps /ˌfrʌnt ˈsteps/ 39-19

front walk /ˌfrʌnt ˈwɔk/ 39-12
frown /fraʊn/ 28-18
frozen dinner /ˌfroʷzən ˈdɪnər/ 13-10
frozen foods /ˌfroʷzən ˈfuʷdz/ 13-B
frozen orange juice /ˌfroʷzən ˈɔrɪndʒ dʒuʷs/ 13-11
frozen vegetables /ˌfroʷzən ˈvedʒtəbəlz/ 13-9
fruit /fruʷt/ 15
fruit cocktail /ˌfruʷt ˈkakteʸl/ 17-2
fruit cup /ˌfruʷt ˈkʌp/ 17-2
frying pan /ˌfraɪ-ɪŋ ˈpæn/ 46-5
fuel gauge /ˈfyuʷəl ˌgeʸdʒ/ 55-15
fuel tank /ˈfyuʷəl ˌtæŋk/ 77-15
full /fʊl/ 34-31
fullback /ˈfʊlbæk/ 65-28
furious /ˈfyʊəriʸəs/ 32-11
furrow /ˈfɜroʷ/ 73-13

Gabon /gəˈboʷn/ 8
galaxy /ˈgæləksiʸ/ 77-1
gall bladder /ˈgɔl ˌblædər/ 24-58
Gambia /ˈgæmbiʸə/ 8
games /geʸmz/ 79-C
garage /gəˈraʒ/ 39-3
garage door /gəˌraʒ ˈdɔr/ 39-2
garden /ˈgardn/ 40
garlic /ˈgarlɪk/ 16-19
garlic press /ˈgarlɪk ˌpres/ 46-26
gas pedal /ˈgæs ˌpedl/ 55-22
gas pump /ˈgæs ˌpʌmp/ 55-2
gas station /ˈgæs ˌsteʸʃən/ 55-1
gate /geʸt/ 59-7; 66-72
gauze /gɔz/ 29-25
gearshift /ˈgɪərʃɪft/ 55-23
gems /dʒemz/ 38-C
George Washington's Birthday /ˌdʒɔrdʒ ˌwaʃɪŋtənz ˈbɜrθdeʸ/ 3-3
Georgia /ˈdʒɔrdʒə/ 9
geranium /dʒəˈreʸniʸəm/ 40-24
gerbil /ˈdʒɜrbəl/ 72-46
get dressed /ˌget ˈdrest/ 26-7
get up /ˌget ˈʌp/ 26-2
Ghana /ˈganə/ 8
gill /gɪl/ 74-8
ginger /ˈdʒɪndʒər/ 16-27
giraffe /dʒəˈræf/ 71-21
girder /ˈgɜrdər/ 53-3
give /gɪv/ 28-4
glove /glʌv/ 37-5; 65-25; 66-52, 67; 68-45
go down /ˌgoʷ ˈdaʊn/ 28-22
go to bed /ˌgoʷ tə ˈbed/ 26-21
go up /ˌgoʷ ˈʌp/ 28-19
goal /goʷl/ 66-45, 49
goalie /ˈgoʷliʸ/ 66-50
goat /goʷt/ 73-26
gold /goʷld/ 38-17
goldfish /ˈgoʷldˌfɪʃ/ 72-51
golf /galf/ 67-F
golf ball /ˈgalf ˌbɔl/ 67-19
golf club /ˈgalf ˌklʌb/ 67-18
golfer /ˈgalfər/ 67-17
good /gʊd/ 33-11
gorilla /gəˈrɪlə/ 71-29
Grand Canyon /ˌgrænd ˈkænyən/ 9
grandchildren /ˈgrænˌtʃɪldrən/ 31

granddaughter /ˈgrænˌdɔtər/ 31
grandfather /ˈgrænˌfaðər/ 31
grandmother /ˈgrænˌmʌðər/ 31
grandparents /ˈgrænˌpeərənts/ 31
grandson /ˈgrænsʌn/ 31
grapefruits /ˈgreʸpfruʷts/ 15-15
grapes /greʸps/ 15-3
grass /græs/ 40-3; 54-7
grater /ˈgreʸtər/ 46-27
gray /greʸ/ 35-22
Great Britain /ˌgreʸt ˈbrɪtn/ 8
Great Salt Lake /ˌgreʸt sɔlt ˈleʸk/ 9
Greece /griʸs/ 8
green /griʸn/ 35-23; 67-21
green beans /ˌgriʸn ˈbiʸnz/ 16-21; 17-15
Greenland /ˈgriʸnlənd/ 7
Greenland Sea /ˌgriʸnlənd ˈsiʸ/ 8
green onions /ˌgriʸn ˈʌnyənz/ 16-2
green peppers /ˌgriʸn ˈpepərz/ 16-9
grieving /ˈgriʸvɪŋ/ 32-8
grocer /ˈgroʷsər/ 21-18
groceries /ˈgroʷsəriʸz/ 13-5
ground meat /ˌgraʊnd ˈmiʸt/ 14-24
Guatemala /ˌgwatəˈmalə/ 7
guest towel /ˈgest ˌtaʊəl/ 44-1
Guinea /ˈgɪniʸ/ 8
Guinea Bissau /ˌgɪniʸ bɪˈsaʊ/ 8
guinea pig /ˈgɪniʸ ˌpɪg/ 72-49
guitar /gɪˈtar/ 70-6
Gulf of Mexico /ˌgʌlf əv ˈmeksikoʷ/ 7; 9
gull /gʌl/ 75-7
gum /gʌm/ 18-17
gutter /ˈgʌtər/ 39-7; 68-36
Guyana /gaɪˈænə/ 7
gym /dʒɪm/ 27

hair /heər/ 23-2
hair brush /ˈheər ˌbrʌʃ/ 25-21
hairdresser /ˈheərˌdresər/ 22-40
hair dryer /ˈheər ˌdraɪər/ 25-22
hair tonic /ˈheər ˌtanɪk/ 25-14
Haiti /ˈheʸtiʸ/ 7
half /hæf/ 1
halfback /ˈhæfbæk/ 65-29
half dollar /ˌhæf ˈdalər/ 6-23
half slip /ˈhæf ˌslɪp/ 36-15
hall /hɔl/ 39-25
Halloween /ˌhæləˈwiʸn/ 3-11
hamburger /ˈhæmˌbɜrgər/ 18-24
hammer /ˈhæmər/ 50-12
hamper /ˈhæmpər/ 49-20
hamster /ˈhæmstər/ 72-48
hand /hænd/ 23-14
handbag /ˈhændbæg/ 36-5
handball /ˈhændbɔl/ 68-M
handball player /ˈhændbɔl ˌpleʸər/ 68-44
hand beater /ˈhænd ˌbiʸtər/ 46-23
hand drill /ˈhænd ˌdrɪl/ 50-31
handkerchief /ˈhæŋkərtʃɪf/ 38-31
handle /ˈhændl/ 43-11; 45-25; 46-6; 56-18

hand towel /ˈhænd ˌtaʊəl/ 44-3
hangar /ˈhæŋər/ 60-47
hanger /ˈhæŋər/ 49-25
happy /ˈhæpiʸ/ 32-2
harbor /ˈharbər/ 61-1
hard /hard/ 34-44
hard hat /ˈhard ˌhæt/ 53-5
harmonica /harˈmanɪkə/ 70-22
hat /hæt/ 37-4; 62-15
hatchet /ˈhætʃɪt/ 50-33
Hawaii /həˈwaɪ-iʸ/ 9
hawk /hɔk/ 75-16
head /hed/ 23-24
headache /ˈhedeʸk/ 29-9
headboard /ˈhedbɔrd/ 43-2
headphone /ˈhedfoʷn/ 51-19
heart /hart/ 24-56
heat control /ˈhiʸt kənˌtroʷl/ 43-20
heater /ˈhiʸtər/ 55-19
heater hose /ˈhiʸtər ˌhoʷz/ 55-25
heavy /ˈheviʸ/ 33-8
hedge /hedʒ/ 40-14
heel /hiʸl/ 23-36; 37-14
height /haɪt/ 5-6
helicopter /ˈhelɪˌkaptər/ 60-46; 78-13
helmet /ˈhelmɪt/ 64-17; 65-21; 67-4
hen /hen/ 73-28
hero /ˈhɪəroʷ/ 18-1
high /haɪ/ 33-3
highchair /ˈhaɪtʃeər/ 47-16
highway /ˈhaɪweʸ/ 57-A
hiker /ˈhaɪkər/ 67-22
hiking /ˈhaɪkɪŋ/ 67-G
hiking boot /ˈhaɪkɪŋ ˌbuʷt/ 67-24
hill /hɪl/ 54-5
hill sign /ˈhɪl ˌsaɪn/ 58-36
hip /hɪp/ 23-31
hippopotamus /ˌhɪpəˈpatəməs/ 71-13
hobbies /ˈhabiʸz/ 79-A
hockey player /ˈhakiʸ ˌpleʸər/ 66-48
hockey stick /ˈhakiʸ ˌstɪk/ 66-55
hole /hoʷl/ 67-20
holidays /ˈhalədeʸz/ 3-D
home /hoʷm/ 26; 65-15
home plate /ˈhoʷm ˌpleʸt/ 65-15
Honduras /hanˈdʊərəs/ 7
honeycomb /ˈhʌniʸˌkoʷm/ 76-2
honeydew melons /ˌhʌniʸˈduʷ ˈmelənz/ 15-24
hook /hʊk/ 50-4; 53-2; 80-16
hop /hap/ 27-7
horn /hɔrn/ 71-12
horse /hɔrs/ 67-9; 73-16
horseback rider /ˈhɔrsbæk ˌraɪdər/ 67-8
horseback riding /ˈhɔrsbæk ˌraɪdɪŋ/ 67-D
horse racing /ˈhɔrs ˌreʸsɪŋ/ 66-J
hose /hoʷz/ 55-4
hot /hat/ 4-a; 34-27
hot dog /ˈhat ˌdɔg/ 18-25
hotel /hoʷˈtel/ 62-1
hot water faucet /ˌhat ˈwɔtər ˌfɔsɪt/ 44-22
hour hand /ˈaʊər ˌhænd/ 2-b
housing /ˈhaʊzɪŋ/ 39
hubcap /ˈhʌbkæp/ 55-34
Hudson Bay /ˌhʌdsən ˈbeʸ/ 7
hummingbird /ˈhʌmɪŋˌbɜrd/ 75-26

hump /hʌmp/ **71**-20
Hungary /'hʌŋgəriʸ/ **8**
husband /'hʌzbənd/ **31**
hygienist /haɪ'dʒiʸnɪst/ **22**-28
hypotenuse /haɪ'patənuʷs/ **5**-10

ice /aɪs/ **64**-15; **66**-56
ice cream /'aɪs kriʸm/ **17**-21
ice hockey /'aɪs ˌhakiʸ/ **66**-E
Iceland /'aɪslənd/ **7**
ice skating /'aɪs ˌskeʸtɪŋ/ **64**-E
icy /'aɪsiʸ/ **4**-8
Idaho /'aɪdəˌhoʷ/ **9**
ignition /ɪg'nɪʃən/ **55**-18
Illinois /ˌɪlə'nɔɪ/ **9**
in box /'ɪn ˌbaks/ **20**-11
in the morning /ɪn ðə 'mɔrnɪŋ/ **2**-i
inch /ɪntʃ/ **5**-28
Independence Day /ˌɪndɪ'pɛndəns ˌdeʸ/ **3**-9
index file /'ɪndɛks ˌfaɪl/ **20**-3
India /'ɪndiʸə/ **8**
Indiana /ˌɪndiʸ'ænə/ **9**
Indian Ocean /ˌɪndiʸən 'oʷʃən/ **8**
Indonesia /ˌɪndə'niʸʒə/ **8**
infant /'ɪnfənt/ **47**-12
information booth /ˌɪnfər'meʸʃən ˌbuʷθ/ **56**-1
insects /'ɪnsɛkts/ **76**-A
instrument panel /'ɪnstrəmənt ˌpænl/ **55**-13; **60**-25
intersection /ˌɪntər'sɛkʃən/ **58**-F
Iowa /'aɪəwə/ **9**
Iran /ɪ'ran/ **8**
Iraq /ɪ'rak/ **8**
Ireland /'aɪərlənd/ **8**
iron /'aɪərn/ **49**-1
ironing board /'aɪərnɪŋ ˌbɔrd/ **49**-2
irrigation system /ˌɪrə'geʸʃən ˌsɪstəm/ **73**-15
isosceles triangle /aɪˌsasəliʸz 'traɪˌæŋgəl/ **5**-B
Israel /'ɪzriʸəl/ **8**
Italy /'ɪtəliʸ/ **8**
Ivory Coast /ˌaɪvəriʸ 'koʷst/ **8**

jacket /'dʒækɪt/ **35**-2; **36**-2; **37**-2
jack hammer /'dʒæk ˌhæmər/ **53**-20
Jamaica /dʒə'meʸkə/ **7**
January /'dʒænyuʷˌɛriʸ/ **3**
Japan /dʒə'pæn/ **8**
jeans /dʒiʸnz/ **35**-16; **36**-12
jeep /dʒiʸp/ **78**-7
jello /'dʒɛloʷ/ **17**-22
jet /dʒɛt/ **60**-39
jet engine /'dʒɛt ˌɛndʒən/ **60**-41
jet plane /'dʒɛt ˌpleʸn/ **60**-39
jewelry /'dʒuʷəlriʸ/ **38**-A
Jockey shorts /'dʒakiʸ ˌʃɔrts/ **35**-18
jogger /'dʒagər/ **67**-1
jogging /'dʒagɪŋ/ **67**-A
Jordan /'dʒɔrdn/ **8**
journalist /'dʒɜrnl-ɪst/ **22**-33
July /dʒʊ'laɪ/ **3**
June /dʒuʷn/ **3**

jungle gym /'dʒʌŋgəl ˌdʒɪm/ **48**-7

Kampuchea /ˌkæmpuʷ'tʃiʸə/ **8**
kangaroo /ˌkæŋgə'ruʷ/ **71**-26
Kansas /'kænzəs/ **9**
karate /kə'ratiʸ/ **66**-H
kayak /'kaɪæk/ **63**-32
kayaker /'kaɪækər/ **63**-31
kayaking /'kaɪækɪŋ/ **63**-L
Kentucky /kən'tʌkiʸ/ **9**
Kenya /'kɛnyə/ **8**
ketchup /'kɛtʃəp/ **18**-7
keyboard /'kiʸbɔrd/ **52**-26
key ring /'kiʸ ˌrɪŋ/ **38**-11
kick /kɪk/ **27**-16
kid /kɪd/ **73**-27
kitchen /'kɪtʃən/ **39**-26; **45**
kitchenware /'kɪtʃənˌwɛər/ **46**
kite /kaɪt/ **48**-18
kitten /'kɪtn/ **72**-41
kiwis /'kiʸwiʸz/ **15**-4
Kleenex /'kliʸnɛks/ **29**-14
knee /niʸ/ **23**-18
kneel /niʸl/ **27**-5
knee sock /'niʸ ˌsak/ **36**-19
knife /naɪf/ **42**-12; **45**-27; **46**-24
knitting /'nɪtɪŋ/ **79**-17
knitting needle /'nɪtɪŋ ˌniʸdl/ **79**-18; **80**-5
koala bear /koʷ'alə ˌbɛər/ **71**-25
Kuwait /kuʷ'weʸt/ **8**

Labor Day /'leʸbər ˌdeʸ/ **3**-10
Labrador Sea /ˌlæbrədɔr 'siʸ/ **10**
ladder /'lædər/ **53**-4
ladle /'leʸdl/ **46**-22
ladybug /'leʸdiʸˌbʌg/ **76**-8
lake /leʸk/ **54**-12
Lake Erie /leʸk 'ɪəriʸ/ **9**
Lake Huron /leʸk 'hyʊərən/ **9**
Lake Michigan /leʸk 'mɪʃɪgən/ **9**
Lake Ontario /leʸk an'tɛəriʸoʷ/ **9**
Lake Superior /leʸk sə'pɪəriʸər/ **9**
lamb /læm/ **73**-25
lamb chops /'læm ˌtʃaps/ **14**-26
lamp /læmp/ **20**-2; **41**-8; **43**-8; **47**-6
lamp shade /'læmp ˌʃeʸd/ **41**-9
land /lænd/ **54**
Laos /'laoʷs/ **8**
lapel /lə'pɛl/ **35**-4
large intestine /ˌlardʒ ɪn'tɛstɪn/ **24**-60
laugh /læf/ **28**-15
laundry /'lɔndriʸ/ **49**-19
laundry bag /'lɔndriʸ ˌbæg/ **49**-21
laundry basket /'lɔndriʸ ˌbæskət/ **49**-22
laundry room /'lɔndriʸ ˌruʷm/ **49**
lawn /lɔn/ **39**-11; **40**-3
lawn mower /'lɔn ˌmoʷər/ **40**-4
leaf /liʸf/ **40**-2
Lebanon /'lɛbənən/ **8**
leeks /liʸks/ **16**-30
left end /'lɛft ˌɛnd/ **65**-38
left guard /'lɛft ˌgard/ **65**-36

left lane /ˌlɛft 'leʸn/ **57**-7
left tackle /'lɛft ˌtækəl/ **65**-37
leg /lɛg/ **23**-18
lemons /'lɛmənz/ **15**-13
length /lɛŋkθ/ **5**-15
lens /lɛnz/ **52**-40
leopard /'lɛpərd/ **71**-6
Lesotho /lə'suʷtuʷ/ **8**
letter carrier /'lɛtər ˌkæriʸər/ **21**-14
lettuce /'lɛtɪs/ **16**-1
level /'lɛvəl/ **50**-27; **53**-18
Liberia /laɪ'bɪəriʸə/ **8**
license plate /'laɪsəns ˌpleʸt/ **55**-8
lid /lɪd/ **46**-2
lie down /ˌlaɪ 'daʊn/ **27**-4
lifeguard /'laɪfgard/ **62**-11
lifeguard stand /'laɪfgard ˌstænd/ **62**-10
life jacket /'laɪf ˌdʒækɪt/ **63**-34
lift /lɪft/ **27**-14
light /laɪt/ **33**-7; **34**-35; **39**-10
light bulb /'laɪt ˌbʌlb/ **49**-28
light switch /'laɪt swɪtʃ/ **44**-10
limes /laɪmz/ **15**-14
line /laɪn/ **61**-12; **63**-13
lines /laɪnz/ **5**-J
lion /'laɪən/ **71**-1
lip /lɪp/ **23**-7
lipstick /'lɪpˌstɪk/ **25**-8
listen /'lɪsən/ **26**-18
liver /'lɪvər/ **24**-57
living room /'lɪvɪŋ ˌruʷm/ **39**-30; **41**
lizard /'lɪzərd/ **72**-25
llama /'lamə/ **71**-24
loafer /'loʷfər/ **37**-17
lobby /'labiʸ/ **39**-20
lobster /'labstər/ **74**-21
long /lɔŋ/ **33**-9
longshoreman /ˌlɔŋ'ʃɔrmən/ **61**-14
loom /luʷm/ **79**-20
loose /luʷs/ **33**-5
loose-leaf binder /ˌluʷsliʸf ˌbaɪndər/ **80**-20
loose-leaf paper /ˌluʷs liʸf ˌpeʸpər/ **80**-21
Louisiana /luʷˌiʸzi'ænə/ **9**
lounge chair /'laʊndʒ ˌtʃɛər/ **40**-5; **62**-9
love seat /'lʌv siʸt/ **41**-5
low /loʷ/ **33**-4
luggage /'lʌgɪdʒ/ **59**-15
luggage carousel /'lʌgɪdʒ kærəˌsɛl/ **59**-16
luggage carrier /'lʌgɪdʒ ˌkæriʸər/ **59**-14
luggage compartment /'lʌgɪdʒ kəmˌpartmənt/ **56**-14
lunar module /ˌluʷnər 'madʒuʷl/ **77**-11
lunar vehicle /ˌluʷnər 'viʸəkəl/ **77**-12
lung /lʌŋ/ **24**-55

macaroni /ˌmækə'roʷniʸ/ **14**-31
machine gun /mə'ʃiʸn ˌgʌn/ **78**-6
Mackenzie Mountains /məˌkɛnziʸ 'maʊntnz/ **10**
Mackenzie River /məˌkɛnziʸ 'rɪvər/ **10**

mad /mæd/ **32**-10
Madagascar /ˌmædə'gæskər/ **8**
magnifying glass /'mægnəfaɪ-ɪŋ ˌglæs/ **79**-5
mailbag /'meʸlbæg/ **19**-8
mailbox /'meʸlbaks/ **19**-9; **39**-18
mail carrier /'meʸl ˌkæriʸər/ **19**-7
mail slot /'meʸl ˌslat/ **19**-5
mail truck /'meʸl ˌtrʌk/ **19**-6
main courses /'meʸn ˌkɔrsɪz/ **17**-C
Maine /meʸn/ **9**
Malawi /mə'lawiʸ/ **8**
Malaysia /mə'leʸʒə/ **8**
Mali /'maliʸ/ **8**
mane /meʸn/ **71**-2; **73**-17
mangoes /'mæŋgoʷz/ **15**-5
Manitoba /ˌmænɪ'toʷbə/ **10**
mantel /'mæntl/ **41**-21
March /martʃ/ **3**
margarine /'mardʒərɪn/ **13**-15
marines /mə'riʸnz/ **78**-D
Maritime Provinces /'mærətaɪm ˌpravɪnsɪz/ **10**
marquee /mar'kiʸ/ **69**-19
Maryland /'mɛərɪlənd/ **9**
mascara /mæ'skærə/ **25**-6
mask /mæsk/ **63**-10; **65**-24; **66**-51
masking tape /'mæskɪŋ ˌteʸp/ **80**-32
mason /'meʸsən/ **21**-2
Massachusetts /ˌmæsə'tʃuʷsɪts/ **9**
mast /mæst/ **63**-20
mat /mæt/ **66**-64
material /mə'tɪəriʸəl/ **80**-8
mattress /'mætrɪs/ **43**-21
Mauritania /ˌmɔrə'teʸniʸə/ **8**
May /meʸ/ **3**
meadow /'mɛdoʷ/ **54**-3
measurements /'mɛʒərmənts/ **5**-K
measuring cup /'mɛʒərɪŋ ˌkʌp/ **46**-12; **49**-18
measuring spoon /'mɛʒərɪŋ ˌspuʷn/ **46**-13
meat /miʸt/ **14**-E
meatballs /'miʸtbɔlz/ **17**-13
mechanic /mɪ'kænɪk/ **21**-8
medicine /'mɛdəsən/ **29**-B
medicine cabinet /'mɛdəsən ˌkæbənɪt/ **44**-15
Mediterranean Sea /ˌmɛdɪtəreʸniʸən 'siʸ/ **8**
Memorial Day /mə'mɔriʸəl ˌdeʸ/ **3**-7
men's wear /'mɛnz ˌwɛər/ **35**; **37**
menu /'mɛnyuʷ/ **17**
message pad /'mɛsɪdʒ ˌpæd/ **20**-22
messy /'mɛsiʸ/ **33**-2
metals /'mɛtlz/ **38**-B
meter /'miʸtər/ **5**-25, 27
Mexico /'mɛksɪkoʷ/ **7**
Michigan /'mɪʃɪgən/ **9**
microwave oven /'maɪkrəweʸv ˌʌvən/ **46**-15
Middle Atlantic States /ˌmɪdl ət.læntɪk 'steʸts/ **9**
middle lane /ˌmɪdl 'leʸn/ **57**-8
middle seat /ˌmɪdl 'siʸt/ **60**-32

midnight /'mɪdnaɪt/ **2**-g
Midwest /mɪd'wɛst/ **9**
Midwestern States
/ˌmɪdwɛstərn 'steˁts/ **9**
military /'mɪləˌteriˁ/ **78**
milk /mɪlk/ **13**-17
milk shake /'mɪlk ʃeˁk/ **18**-19
Minnesota /ˌmɪnɪ'soˁtə/ **9**
minus /'maɪnəs/ **1**
minus twenty /ˌmaɪnəs 'twɛnti/
4-g
minus twenty degrees
/ˌmaɪnəs twɛnti dɪ'griˁz/ **4**-g
minute hand /'mɪnɪt ˌhænd/
2-c
mirror /'mɪrər/ **30**-9; **42**-21;
43-12; **44**-14
miserable /'mɪzərəbəl/ **32**-7
missing tooth /ˌmɪsɪŋ 'tuˁθ/
30-16
Mississippi /ˌmɪsɪ'sɪpiˁ/ **9**
Mississippi River
/ˌmɪsɪsɪpiˁ 'rɪvər/ **9**
Missouri /mɪ'zʊəriˁ/ **9**
Missouri River
/mɪˌzʊəriˁ 'rɪvər/ **9**
mitt /mɪt/ **65**-25
mixer /'mɪksər/ **46**-20
model /'mɑdl/ **22**-44
Monday /'mʌndiˁ/ **3**
money /'mʌniˁ/ **6**
money clip /'mʌniˁ ˌklɪp/ **38**-10
money order /'mʌniˁ ˌɔrdər/
6-18
Mongolia /mɑŋ'goˁliˁə/ **8**
monitor /'mɑnətər/ **52**-4
monkey /'mʌŋkiˁ/ **71**-28
Monopoly /mə'nɑpəliˁ/ **79**-31
Montana /mɑn'tænə/ **9**
monthly statement
/ˌmʌnθliˁ 'steˁtmənt/ **6**-14
months /mʌnθs/ **3**-B
Moon /muˁn/ **77**-7
mop /mɑp/ **49**-10, 11, 12
Morocco /mə'rɑkoˁ/ **8**
mosquito /mə'skiˁtoˁ/ **76**-4
mother /'mʌðər/ **31**
mother-in-law /'mʌðər ɪn ˌlɔ/
31
Mother's Day /'mʌðərz ˌdeˁ/
3-6
motorboat /'moˁtərˌboˁt/ **63**-24
mound /maʊnd/ **65**-4
mountain /'maʊntn/ **54**-1
mouse /maʊs/ **76**-1
mouth /maʊθ/ **23**-6
mouthwash /'maʊθwɑʃ/ **30**-14
movie theater
/'muˁviˁ ˌθiˁətər/ **69**-E
Mozambique /ˌmoˁzɑm'biˁk/ **8**
music /'myuˁzɪk/ **69**-4
musical instruments
/ˌmyuˁzɪkəl 'ɪnstrəmənts/ **70**
music stand /'myuˁzɪk ˌstænd/
69-5
mussel /'mʌsəl/ **74**-23
mustache /'mʌstæʃ, mə'stæʃ/
24-47
mustard /'mʌstərd/ **18**-6

nail /neˁl/ **23**-17; **50**-2
nail clipper /'neˁl ˌklɪpər/ **25**-17
nail file /'neˁl faɪl/ **25**-18
nail polish /'neˁl ˌpɑlɪʃ/ **25**-20
Namibia /nə'mɪbiˁə/ **8**

napkin /'næpkɪn/ **18**-22; **42**-5
napkin ring /'næpkɪn rɪŋ/ **42**-4
narrow /'næroˁ/ **34**-40
navy /'neˁviˁ/ **78**-C
neat /niˁt/ **33**-1
Nebraska /nə'bræskə/ **9**
neck /nɛk/ **23**-25
necklace /'nɛk-lɪs/ **38**-7
nectarines /'nɛktəriˁnz/ **15**-9
needle /'niˁdl/ **80**-12
Nepal /nə'pɑl/ **8**
nephew /'nɛfyuˁ/ **31**
nervous /'nɜrvəs/ **32**-16
nest /nɛst/ **75**-31
net /nɛt/ **66**-60; **68**-30, 42
Netherlands /'nɛðərləndz/ **8**
Nevada /nɪ'vædə/ **9**
new /nuˁ/ **34**-33
New Brunswick
/nuˁ 'brʌnzwɪk/ **10**
New England /nuˁ 'ɪŋglənd/ **9**
Newfoundland /'nuˁfəndlənd/
10
New Hampshire
/nuˁ 'hæmpʃər/ **9**
New Jersey /nuˁ 'dʒɜrziˁ/ **9**
New Mexico /nuˁ 'mɛksɪkoˁ/ **9**
new potatoes /nuˁ pə'teˁtoˁz/
16-11
newscaster /'nuˁzˌkæstər/ **22**-32
newsstand /'nuˁzstænd/ **12**-21
New Year's Day
/ˌnuˁ yɪərz 'deˁ/ **3**-1
New York /nuˁ 'yɔrk/ **9**
New Zealand /nuˁ 'ziˁlənd/ **8**
Nicaragua /ˌnɪkə'rɑgwə/ **7**
nickel /'nɪkəl/ **6**-20
niece /niˁs/ **31**
Niger /'naɪdʒər/ **8**
Nigeria /naɪ'dʒɪəriˁə/ **8**
nightgown /'naɪtgaʊn/ **37**-23
nightstand /'naɪtstænd/ **43**-1
night table /naɪt ˌteˁbəl/ **43**-1
nightwear /'naɪtwɛər/ **37**-E
nipple /'nɪpəl/ **47**-20
no left turn sign
/noˁ lɛft 'tɜrn ˌsaɪn/ **58**-33
noon /nuˁn/ **2**-h
no right turn sign
/noˁ raɪt 'tɜrn ˌsaɪn/ **58**/34
north /nɔrθ/ **9**
North America
/ˌnɔrθ ə'mɛrɪkə/ **7**
North Carolina
/ˌnɔrθ kærə'laɪnə/ **9**
North Dakota /ˌnɔrθ də'koˁtə/ **9**
Northern Canada
/ˌnɔrðərn 'kænədə/ **10**
North Korea /ˌnɔrθ kə'riˁə/ **8**
Northwest Territories
/ˌnɔrθwɛst 'tɛrəˌtɔriˁz/ **10**
Norway /'nɔrweˁ/ **8**
nose /noˁz/ **23**-5
notebook /'noˁtbʊk/ **80**-19
note pad /'noˁt ˌpæd/ **20**-21
no trucks sign
/noˁ 'trʌks ˌsaɪn/ **58**-35
no U-turn sign
/noˁ 'yuˁ tɜrn ˌsaɪn/ **58**-32
Nova Scotia /ˌnoˁvə 'skoˁʃə/ **10**
November /noˁ'vɛmbər/ **3**
Novocain /'noˁvəˌkeˁn/ **30**-10
nozzle /'nɑzəl/ **55**-3
numbers /'nʌmbərz/ **1**
nurse /nɜrs/ **22**-26; **29**-1
nursery /'nɜrsəriˁ/ **47**

nut /nʌt/ **50**-5

oar /ɔr/ **63**-27
oboe /'oˁboˁ/ **70**-13
obtuse angle /əbˌtuˁs 'æŋgəl/
5-7
occupations /ˌɑkyə'peˁʃənz/ **21**
ocean /'oˁʃən/ **62**-13
ocean liner /ˌoˁʃən 'laɪnər/
61-3
October /ɑk'toˁbər/ **3**
octopus /'ɑktəpəs/ **74**-12
off-duty sign /ɔf 'duˁtiˁ ˌsaɪn/
56-17
office /'ɔfɪs/ **20**
office building /'ɔfɪs ˌbɪldɪŋ/
11-18
Ohio /oˁ'haɪoˁ/ **9**
oil tanker /'ɔɪl ˌtæŋkər/ **61**-16
Oklahoma /ˌoˁklə'hoˁmə/ **9**
old /oˁld/ **33**-16; **34**-34
Oman /oˁ'mɑn/ **8**
on board /ɑn 'bɔrd/ **60**-B
one way sign /ˌwʌn weˁ 'saɪn/
11-17
one way traffic sign
/ˌwʌn weˁ 'træfɪk ˌsaɪn/ **11**-17
onion rings /'ʌnyən ˌrɪŋz/ **18**-26
onions /'ʌnyənz/ **16**-14; **18**-10
Ontario /ɑn'tɛəriˁoˁ/ **10**
open /'oˁpən/ **34**-29
opera /'ɑpərə/ **69**-B
opposites /'ɑpəzɪts/ **33**
optometrist /ɑp'tɑmətrɪst/
22-29
orange /'ɔrɪndʒ/ **36**-25
oranges /'ɔrɪndʒɪz/ **15**-16
orchestra /'ɔrkɪstrə/ **69**-1
orchestra pit /'ɔrkɪstrə ˌpɪt/
69-18
Oregon /'ɔrɪgən/ **9**
ostrich /'ɔstrɪtʃ/ **75**-13
ottoman /'ɑtəmən/ **41**-25
out box /'aʊt ˌbɑks/ **20**-12
outerwear /'aʊtərˌwɛər/ **37**-A
outfielder /'aʊtˌfiˁldər/ **65**-8
outlet /'aʊtlɛt/ **49**-27
oval /'oˁvəl/ **5**-G
oven /'ʌvən/ **45**-1
over /'oˁvər/ **34**-47
overalls /'oˁvərˌɔlz/ **48**-12
overhead compartment
/ˌoˁvərhɛd kəm'pɑrtmənt/
60-27
overhead luggage compartment
/ˌoˁvərhɛd 'lʌgɪdʒ
kəmˌpɑrtmənt/ **60**-27
overpass /'oˁvərˌpæs/ **57**-1
owl /aʊl/ **75**-18

Pacific Coast States
/pəˌsɪfɪk 'koˁst ˌsteˁts/ **9**
Pacific Ocean
/pəˌsɪfɪk 'oˁʃən/ **7**; **8**; **9**; **10**
pack /pæk/ **67**-6
package /'pækɪdʒ/ **19**-2
packaged goods
/'pækɪdʒd ˌgʊdz/ **14**-F
packer /'pækər/ **13**-6
paddle /'pædl/ **63**-30; **69**-40
pail /peˁl/ **48**-10; **49**-13; **62**-18
paint /peˁnt/ **28**-10; **50**-16
paintbrush /'peˁntˌbrʌʃ/ **50**-15
paint can /'peˁnt ˌkæn/ **50**-19

painter /'peˁntər/ **21**-4
painting /'peˁntɪŋ/ **79**-23
paint roller /'peˁnt ˌroˁlər/ **50**-17
pair of scissors
/ˌpɛər əv 'sɪzərz/ **80**-6
paisley /'peˁzliˁ/ **35**-29
pajamas /pə'dʒɑməz/ **37**-24
Pakistan /'pækɪstæn/ **8**
palm /pɑm/ **23**-33
pan /pæn/ **50**-10
Panama /'pænəmə/ **7**
pansy /'pænziˁ/ **40**-23
panties /'pæntiˁz/ **36**-17
pants /pænts/ **35**-12; **36**-9
panty hose /'pæntiˁ ˌhoˁz/ **36**-20
papayas /pə'paɪəz/ **15**-18
paper /'peˁpər/ **80**-21
paper clip /'peˁpər ˌklɪp/ **20**-29
paper clip holder
/'peˁpər klɪp ˌhoˁldər/ **20**-13
paper napkin /ˌpeˁpər 'næpkɪn/
18-22
paper plate /ˌpeˁpər 'pleˁt/
18-23
Papua New Guinea
/ˌpæpuˁə nuˁ 'gɪniˁ/ **8**
parachute /'pærəˌʃuˁt/ **78**-11
parachutist /'pærəˌʃuˁtɪst/ **78**-12
Paraguay /'pærəgwaɪ/ **7**
parakeet /'pærəˌkiˁt/ **72**-45
parallel /'pærəlɛl/ **5**-22
parcel /'pɑrsəl/ **19**-2
parents /'pɛərənts/ **31**
paring knife /'pɛərɪŋ ˌnaɪf/
45-27
parking lot /'pɑrkɪŋ ˌlɑt/ **11**-5
parking meter
/'pɑrkɪŋ ˌmiˁtər/ **11**-6
parrot /'pærət/ **72**-44
parsnips /'pɑrsnɪps/ **16**-28
passenger /'pæsəndʒər/
12-27; **56**-10; **60**-29
passenger car
/'pæsəndʒər ˌkɑr/ **56**-8
passenger ship
/'pæsəndʒər ˌʃɪp/ **61**-3
passport /'pæspɔrt/ **59**-21
patient /'peˁʃənt/ **29**-4; **30**-2
patio /'pætiˁˌoˁ/ **40**-8
patio chair /'pætiˁoˁ ˌtʃɛər/
40-11
patio table /'pætiˁoˁ ˌteˁbəl/
40-10
patterns /'pætərnz/ **35**-E; **36**-E
paw /pɔ/ **71**-4; **72**-40
peaches /'piˁtʃɪz/ **15**-19; **17**-16
peacock /'piˁkɑk/ **75**-19
peak /piˁk/ **54**-2
peanuts /'piˁnʌts/ **18**-15
pearl onions /'pɜrl ˌʌnyənz/
16-16
pearls /pɜrlz/ **38**-8
pears /pɛərz/ **15**-2
pedestrian /pə'dɛstriˁən/ **11**-11
pediatrician /ˌpiˁdiˁə'trɪʃən/
22-25
peeler /'piˁlər/ **46**-30
pelican /'pɛlɪkən/ **75**-2
pen /pɛn/ **20**-25
pencil /'pɛnsəl/ **20**-26; **80**-22
pencil holder
/'pɛnsəl ˌhoˁldər/ **20**-4
pencil sharpener
/'pɛnsəl ˌʃɑrpənər/ **20**-5; **80**-23
penguin /'pɛŋgwɪn/ **75**-10
Pennsylvania /ˌpɛnsəl'veˁnyə/ **9**

penny /'pɛniʸ/ 6-19
percent /pər'sɛnt/ 1
percussion /pər'kʌʃən/ 70-D
perpendicular /ˌpɜrpən'dıkyələr/ 5-21
personal cassette player /ˌpɜrsənəl kə'sɛt ˌpleʸər/ 51-18
Peru /pə'ruʷ/ 7
pets /pɛts/ 72-B
pharmacist /'farməsıst/ 22-31
pheasant /'fɛzənt/ 75-22
Philippines /'fıləpiʸnz/ 8
phone booth /'foʷn ˌbuʷθ/ 11-15
photocopier /'foʷtəˌkapiʸər/ 20-31
photographer /fə'tagrəfər/ 22-45
photography /fə'tagrəfiʸ/ 79-10
piano /piʸ'ænoʷ/ 70-20
pickax /'pık-æks/ 53-23
pickles /'pıkəlz/ 18-9
pick up /ˌpık 'ʌp/ 28-9
pick-up truck /'pık ʌp ˌtrʌk/ 55-38
picture /'pıktʃər/ 41-22
picture frame /'pıktʃər ˌfreʸm/ 41-23
picture postcard /ˌpıktʃər 'poʷstkard/ 19-19
pier /pıər/ 61-2
pig /pıg/ 73-18
pigeon /'pıdʒən/ 75-21
piglet /'pıglıt/ 73-19
pigpen /'pıgpɛn/ 73-20
pig sty /'pıg ˌstaı/ 73-20
pillow /'pıloʷ/ 41-3; 43-15
pillowcase /'pıloʷˌkeʸs/ 43-14
pilot /'paılət/ 60-23; 78-10
pin /pın/ 38-9; 68-38
pin cushion /'pın ˌkuʃən/ 80-9
pineapples /'paınˌæpəlz/ 15-17
ping pong /'pıŋ paŋ/ 68-L
ping pong ball /'pıŋ paŋ ˌbɔl/ 68-41
ping pong player /'pıŋ paŋ ˌpleʸər/ 68-39
ping pong table /'pıŋ paŋ ˌteʸbəl/ 68-43
pink /pıŋk/ 36-22
pitcher /'pıtʃər/ 65-5
pitcher's mound /'pıtʃərz ˌmaʊnd/ 65-4
pizza /'piʸtsə/ 18-3
plaid /plæd/ 35-31
plane /pleʸn/ 50-26
planet /'plænıt/ 77-5
plant /plænt/ 41-15
planter /'plæntər/ 41-16
plastic wrap /ˌplæstık 'ræp/ 45-29
plate /pleʸt/ 18-23; 42-6; 45-22
platform /'plætfɔrm/ 56-7
player /'pleʸər/ 66-40, 44, 48, 57; 68-28, 39, 44, 46, 49
playground /'pleʸˌgraʊnd/ 48
playpen /'pleʸˌpɛn/ 47-17
pleased /pliʸzd/ 32-1
pliers /'plaıərz/ 50-10
plug converter /'plʌg kənˌvɜrtər/ 52-34
plumber /'plʌmər/ 21-11
plums /plʌmz/ 15-10
plus /plʌs/ 1
P.M. /ˌpiʸ 'ɛm/ 2-j

pneumatic drill /nʊˌmætık 'drıl/ 53-20
pocket /'pakıt/ 35-10
pocket calculator /ˌpakıt 'kælkyəˌleʸtər/ 52-28
podium /'poʷdiʸəm/ 69-2
point /pɔınt/ 28-16
Poland /'poʷlənd/ 8
polar bear /'poʷlər ˌbɛər/ 71-15
pole /poʷl/ 64-3
police officer /pə'liʸs ˌɔfəsər/ 21-13
polka dot /'poʷlkə ˌdat/ 36-31
pond /pand/ 54-13; 73-7
pork chops /'pɔrk 'tʃaps/ 14-22; 17-11
port /pɔrt/ 61-4
porter /'pɔrtər/ 56-9; 59-13
Portugal /'pɔrtʃəgəl/ 8
postal clerk /'poʷstəl ˌklɜrk/ 19-1
postcard /'poʷstkard/ 19-19
post office /'poʷst ˌɔfıs/ 19
pot /pat/ 45-15; 46-3
potato chips /pə'teʸtoʷ ˌtʃıps/ 18-11
pot holder /'pat ˌhoʷldər/ 45-31
potter's wheel /'patərz ˌhwiʸl/ 79-22
pottery /'patəriʸ/ 79-21
pouch /paʊtʃ/ 71-27
poultry /'poʷltriʸ/ 14-E
power saw /'paʊər ˌsɔ/ 50-28
prescription /prı'skrıpʃən/ 29-26
pretty /'prıtiʸ/ 33-19
pretzels /'prɛtsəlz/ 18-13
Prince Edward Island /prıns 'ɛdwərd ˌaılənd/ 10
print /prınt/ 36-29
printer /'prıntər/ 52-27
protractor /proʷ'træktər/ 80-24
proud /praʊd/ 32-20
puck /pʌk/ 66-54
Puerto Rico /ˌpwɛərtə 'riʸkoʷ/ 7
pull /pʊl/ 27-15; 43-11
pupil /'pyuʷpəl/ 24-45
puppy /'pʌpiʸ/ 72-38
purple /'pɜrpəl/ 36-24
push /pʊʃ/ 27-13
put on makeup /ˌpʊt an 'meʸkʌp/ 26-10

Qatar /'katar/ 8
quarter /'kwɔrtər/ 1; 6-22
quarterback /'kwɔrtər ˌbæk/ 65-35
Quebec /kwı'bɛk/ 10
Queen Elizabeth Islands /kwiʸn ı'lızəbəθ ˌaıləndz/ 10
quilt /kwılt/ 43-18

rabbit /'ræbıt/ 72-50
raccoon /ræ'kuʷn/ 71-31
racket /'rækıt/ 66-58; 68-47, 50
racquetball /'rækıtˌbɔl/ 68-O, 51
racquetball player /'rækıtbɔl ˌpleʸər/ 68-49
racquetball racket /'rækıtbɔl ˌrækıt/ 68-50
radar antenna /'reʸdar ænˌtɛnə/ 78-20
radiator /'reʸdiʸˌeʸtər/ 55-32
radio /'reʸdiʸˌoʷ/ 51-15
radio call sign

radio /ˌreʸdiʸoʷ 'kɔl saın/ 56-16
radishes /'rædıˌʃız/ 16-3
radius /'reʸdiʸəs/ 5-20
raft /ræft/ 63-33
railroad crossing /'reʸlroʷd ˌkrɔsıŋ/ 58-G
railroad track /'reʸlroʷd ˌtræk/ 58-25
raincoat /'reʸnkoʷt/ 37-7
rain hat /'reʸn hæt/ 37-8
rainwear /'reʸnwɛər/ 37-B
rainy /'reʸniʸ/ 4-6
rake /'reʸk/ 40-17
ranch house /'ræntʃ haʊs/ 39-B
range /reʸndʒ/ 45-13
rapids /'ræpıdz/ 63-35
rasberries /'ræsˌbɛriʸz/ 15-21
rat /ræt/ 76-13
razor /'reʸzər/ 25-11
razor blade /'reʸzər bleʸd/ 25-12
reach /riʸtʃ/ 27-10
read /riʸd/ 28-8
rear windshield /ˌrıər 'wındʃiʸld/ 55-6
receptionist /rı'sɛpʃənıst/ 20-19
record /'rɛkərd/ 6-10; 51-7
recorder /rı'kɔrdər/ 70-12
rectangle /'rɛkˌtæŋgəl/ 5-E
red /rɛd/ 35-25
redcap /'rɛdkæp/ 56-9
redhead /'rɛdhɛd/ 24-39
red onions /ˌrɛd 'ʌnyənz/ 16-15
red peppers /ˌrɛd 'pɛpərz/ 16-10
Red Sea /ˌrɛd 'siʸ/ 8
referee /ˌrɛfə'riʸ/ 66-69
refrigerator /rı'frıdʒəˌreʸtər/ 45-11
reins /reʸnz/ 67-10
relish /ˌrɛlıʃ/ 18-8
remote control /rıˌmoʷt kən'troʷl/ 51-3
return address /rı'tɜrn əˌdrɛs,-ˌædrɛs/ 19-15
return receipt /rı'tɜrn rıˌsiʸt/ 19-20
rhinoceros /raı'nasərəs/ 71-11
Rhode Island /ˌroʷd 'aılənd/ 9
ribbon /'rıbən/ 80-30
rider /'raıdər/ 67-8
rifle /'raıfəl/ 78-5
right angle /ˌraıt 'æŋgəl/ 5-12
right end /ˌraıt 'ɛnd/ 65-30
right guard /ˌraıt 'gard/ 65-33
right lane /ˌraıt 'leʸn/ 57-9
right tackle /ˌraıt 'tækəl/ 65-32
right triangle /ˌraıt 'traıˌæŋgəl/ 5-3
ring /rıŋ/ 38-4; 66-71
rink /rıŋk/ 66-83
rinse your face /ˌrıns yər 'feʸs/ 26-9
Rio Grande /ˌriʸoʷ 'grænd/ 9
river /'rıvər/ 54-14
roach /roʷtʃ/ 76-5
road /roʷd/ 58-E
road signs /'roʷd ˌsaınz/ 58-H
roast /roʷst/ 14-21
roast beef /'roʷst ˌbiʸf/ 17-9
roast beef sandwich /ˌroʷst biʸf 'sændwıtʃ/ 18-2
roast chicken /ˌroʷst 'tʃıkən/ 17-14
roaster /'roʷstər/ 14-23; 46-7
robe /roʷb/ 37-22
robin /'rabın/ 75-24
rock /rak/ 54-10; 62-20

rock concert /'rak ˌkansɜrt/ 69-F
Rocky Mountains /ˌrakiʸ 'maʊntnz/ 9; 10
Rocky Mountain States /ˌrakiʸ maʊntn 'steʸts/ 9
rodents /'roʷdnts/ 76-B
roll /roʷl/ 17-8
roll of stamps /ˌroʷl əv 'stæmps/ 19-12
roller /'roʷlər/ 50-17
roller skate /'roʷlər ˌskeʸt/ 68-32
roller skater /'roʷlər ˌskeʸtər/ 68-31
rollerskating /'roʷlərˌskeʸtıŋ/ 68-J
rolling pin /'roʷlıŋ ˌpın/ 46-11
Rolodex /'roʷləˌdɛks/ 20-3
Romania /rʊ'meʸniʸə/ 8
roof /ruʷf, rʊf/ 39-4
rooster /'ruʷstər/ 73-30
rope /roʷp/ 66-70
rose /roʷz/ 40-19
rotor /'roʷtər/ 60-45
rouge /ruʷʒ/ 25-2
rough /rʌf/ 34-46
routes /ruʷts/ 57; 58
route sign /'ruʷt ˌsaın/ 58-26
rowboat /'roʷboʷt/ 63-26
rower /'roʷər/ 63-25
rowing /'roʷıŋ/ 63-J
rubber band /ˌrʌbər 'bænd/ 20-28
ruby /'ruʷbiʸ/ 32-22
rug /rʌg/ 41-26; 47-10
ruler /'ruʷlər/ 5-26
run /rʌn/ 27-8
runner /'rʌnər/ 67-2
running /'rʌnıŋ/ 67-B
runningback /'rʌnıŋbæk/ 65-28, 29
runway /'rʌnweʸ/ 60-43
Russia /'rʌʃə/ 8
Rwanda /rʊ'ændə/ 8

sack /sæk/ 13-7
sad /sæd/ 32-6
saddle /'sædl/ 67-11
safe deposit box /ˌseʸf dı'pazıt ˌbaks/ 6-7
safety pin /'seʸftiʸ ˌpın/ 80-11
sail /seʸl/ 63-18
sailboat /'seʸlboʷt/ 63-19
sailing /'seʸlıŋ/ 63-H
sailor /'seʸlər/ 78-17
St. Lawrence River /seʸnt ˌlɔrəns 'rıvər/ 10
St. Patrick's Day /seʸnt 'pætrıks ˌdeʸ/ 3-4
salad /'sæləd/ 17-B, 5
salad fork /'sæləd ˌfɔrk/ 42-10
salesperson /'seʸlzˌpɜrsən/ 22-39
sand /sænd/ 48-9; 62-3
sandal /'sændl/ 37-19
sandbox /'sændbaks/ 48-8
sand castle /'sænd ˌkæsəl/ 62-16
sandpaper /'sændˌpeʸpər/ 50-20
sanitation worker /ˌsænə'teʸʃən ˌwɜrkər/ 21-6
sapphire /'sæfaıər/ 38-23
Saran wrap /sə'ræn ˌræp/ 45-29
Saskatchewan /sæ'skætʃəwan/ 10
satellite /'sætlˌaıt/ 77-13

Saturday /ˈsætərdiʸ/ **3**
Saturn /ˈsætərn/ **77**-5
saucer /ˈsɔsər/ **42**-18; **45**-19
Saudi Arabia /ˌsaʊdiʸ əˈreʸbiʸə/ **8**
saw /sɔ/ **50**-34
saxophone /ˈsæksəˌfoʷn/ **70**-15
scaffold /ˈskæfəld/ **53**-7
scale /skeʸl/ **19**-3; **29**-6; **74**-6
scallions /ˈskælyənz/ **16**-2
scared /skɛərd/ **32**-18
scarf /skɑrf/ **38**-30
schedule /ˈskɛdʒuʷəl/ **56**-D
school /skuʷl/ **28**
school crossing sign
 /ˌskuʷl ˈkrɔsɪŋ ˌsaɪn/ **58**-30
scientist /ˈsaɪəntɪst/ **22**-24
scissors /ˈsɪzərz/ **80**-6
Scotch tape /ˌskatʃ ˈteʸp/ **20**-9
Scrabble /ˈskræbəl/ **79**-30
scratch /skrætʃ/ **29**-23
screen /skriʸn/ **41**-20; **51**-5
screw /skruʷ/ **50**-33
screwdriver /ˈskruʷˌdraɪvər/
 50-11
scrub brush /ˈskrʌb ˌbrʌʃ/ **49**-3
scuba diver /ˈskuʷbə ˌdaɪvər/
 63-7
scuba diving /ˈskuʷbə ˌdaɪvɪŋ/
 63-D
sculpt /skʌlpt/ **28**-11
sculpting /ˈskʌlptɪŋ/ **79**-15
sculpture /ˈskʌlptʃər/ **79**-16
sea animals /ˈsiʸ ˌænəməlz/ **74**-B
seal /siʸl/ **74**-16
seamstress /ˈsiʸmstrɪs/ **22**-43
seashell /ˈsiʸʃɛl/ **62**-19
seasons /ˈsiʸzənz/ **4**-A
seat /siʸt/ **55**-24
second /ˈsɛkənd/ **1**
second base /ˌsɛkənd ˈbeʸs/
 65-10
second baseman
 /ˌsɛkənd ˈbeʸsmæn/ **65**-9
second floor /ˌsɛkənd ˈflɔr/
 39-23
secretary /ˈsɛkrəˌtɛriʸ/ **20**-1;
 22-37
security check
 /sɪˈkyʊərəṭiʸ ˌtʃɛk/ **59**-5
security guard
 /sɪˈkyʊərəṭiʸ ˌgɑrd/ **59**-6
sedan /sɪˈdæn/ **55**-33
see-saw /ˈsiʸ ˌsɔ/ **48**-1
Senegal /ˌsɛnɪˈgɔl/ **8**
September /sɛpˈtɛmbər/ **3**
server /ˈsɜrvər/ **42**-16
serving bowl /ˈsɜrvɪŋ ˌboʷl/
 42-15
sewing /ˈsoʷɪŋ/ **80**-A
sewing basket /ˈsoʷɪŋ ˌbæskɪt/
 80-2
sewing machine
 /ˈsoʷɪŋ məˌʃiʸn/ **80**-1
shampoo /ʃæmˈpuʷ/ **25**-9
shapes /ʃeʸps/ **5**
shark /ʃɑrk/ **74**-1
shave /ʃeʸv/ **26**-6
shaving cream /ˈʃeʸvɪŋ ˌkriʸm/
 25-10
sheep /ʃiʸp/ **73**-24
sheet /ʃiʸt/ **43**-16, 17
sheet of stamps
 /ˌʃiʸt əv ˈstæmps/ **19**-11
sheet music /ˈʃiʸt ˌmyuʷzɪk/
 69-4
shelf /ʃɛlf/ **44**-9

shin /ʃɪn/ **23**-21
shin guard /ˈʃɪn ˌgɑrd/ **65**-26
shirt /ʃɜrt/ **35**-5
shocked /ʃakt/ **32**-5
shoe /ʃuʷ/ **37**-13
shoelace /ˈʃuʷleʸs/ **37**-16
shopper /ˈʃapər/ **13**-1
short /ʃɔrt/ **33**-10, 14
shorts /ʃɔrts/ **36**-14
shortstop /ˈʃɔrtstap/ **65**-11
shoulder /ˈʃoʷldər/ **23**-27;
 57-5
shoulder bag /ˈʃoʷldər ˌbæg/
 36-10
shovel /ˈʃʌvəl/ **48**-11; **53**-21
shower curtain /ˈʃaʊər ˌkɜrtn/
 44-26
shower curtain rod
 /ˈʃaʊər kɜrtn ˌrad/ **44**-25
shower head /ˈʃaʊər ˌhɛd/
 44-24
shrimp /ʃrɪmp/ **74**-22
shrimp cocktail
 /ˌʃrɪmp ˈkakteʸl/ **17**-3
shutter /ˈʃʌtər/ **39**-9
shy /ʃaɪ/ **32**-22
sickness /ˈsɪknɪs/ **29**-B
side /saɪd/ **5**-13
sideboard /ˈsaɪdbɔrd/ **42**-20
side door /ˌsaɪd ˈdɔr/ **39**-5
side table /ˌsaɪd ˈteʸbəl/ **41**-24
sidewalk /ˈsaɪdwɔk/ **12**-28
Sierra Leone /siʸˌɛrə liʸˈoʷn/ **8**
Sierra Nevada Mountains
 /siʸˌɛrə nɪˌvædə ˈmaʊntnz/ **9**
silo /ˈsaɪloʷ/ **73**-4
silver /ˈsɪlvər/ **38**-18
silver dollar /ˌsɪlvər ˈdalər/ **6**-24
Singapore /ˈsɪŋgəpɔr/ **8**
singer /ˈsɪŋər/ **69**-7, 21
sink /sɪŋk/ **44**-21; **45**-6
sister /ˈsɪstər/ **31**
sister-in-law /ˈsɪstər ɪn ˌlɔ/ **31**
sisters /ˈsɪstərz/ **31**
sisters-in-law /ˈsɪstərz ɪn ˌlɔ/ **31**
sit /sɪt/ **27**-3
skate /skeʸt/ **64**-14; **66**-53
skateboard /ˈskeʸtbɔrd/ **48**-17
skater /ˈskeʸtər/ **64**-13
ski /skiʸ/ **64**-5
ski boot /ˈskiʸ ˌbuʷt/ **64**-4
ski cap /ˈskiʸ ˌkæp/ **64**-8
skier /ˈskiʸər/ **64**-2, 7
skillet /ˈskɪlɪt/ **46**-5
skirt /skɜrt/ **36**-3
skycap /ˈskaɪkæp/ **59**-13
skyline /ˈskaɪlaɪn/ **11**-1
skyscraper /ˈskaɪˌskreʸpər/ **11**-2
slacks /slæks/ **35**-12; **36**-9
sled /slɛd/ **64**-1
sledding /ˈslɛdɪŋ/ **64**-A
sledge hammer
 /ˈslɛdʒ ˌhæmər/ **53**-22
sleep /sliʸp/ **26**-22
sleeve /sliʸv/ **35**-3
slide /slaɪd/ **48**-2
slide projector
 /ˈslaɪd prəˌdʒɛktər/ **52**-44
slip /slɪp/ **36**-15
slipper /ˈslɪpər/ **37**-20
slippery when wet sign
 /ˌslɪpəriʸ hwɛn ˈwɛt ˌsaɪn/ **58**-37
slow /sloʷ/ **34**-26
small intestine
 /ˌsmɔl ɪnˈtɛstɪn/ **24**-59
smile /smaɪl/ **28**-14

smooth /smuʷð/ **34**-45
smug /smʌg/ **32**-21
snacks /snæks/ **18**
snake /sneʸk/ **72**-33
snap /snæp/ **80**-18
snapdragon /ˈsnæpˌdrægən/
 40-22
sneaker /ˈsniʸkər/ **37**-18
sneakers /ˈsniʸkərz/ **48**-13
snorkel /ˈsnɔrkəl/ **63**-6
snorkeler /ˈsnɔrkələr/ **63**-5
snorkeling /ˈsnɔrkəlɪŋ/ **63**-C
snout /snaʊt/ **74**-2
snowmobile /ˈsnoʷməˌbiʸl/
 64-18
snowmobiling /ˈsnoʷməˌbiʸlɪŋ/
 64-G
snowy /ˈsnoʷiʸ/ **4**-7
soap /soʷp/ **44**-19
soap dish /ˈsoʷp ˌdɪʃ/ **44**-20
soap dispenser
 /ˈsoʷp dɪˌspɛnsər/ **44**-2
soccer /ˈsakər/ **66**-D
soccer ball /ˈsakər ˌbɔl/ **66**-46
soccer field /ˈsakər ˌfiʸld/ **66**-47
soccer player /ˈsakər ˌpleʸər/
 66-44
sock /sak/ **35**-19; **36**-18
socket /ˈsakɪt/ **49**-27
soda /ˈsoʷdə/ **18**-20
sofa /ˈsoʷfə/ **41**-1
soft /sɔft/ **34**-43
soft drink /ˈsɔft ˌdrɪŋk/ **18**-20
soldier /ˈsoʷldʒər/ **78**-1
sole /soʷl/ **37**-15
solid /ˈsalɪd/ **35**-30
solid line /ˌsalɪd ˈlaɪn/ **57**-4
Somalia /səˈmaliʸə/ **8**
son /sʌn/ **31**
son-in-law /ˈsʌn ɪn ˌlɔ/ **31**
soup /suʷp/ **14**-19; **17**-B, 4
soupspoon /ˈsuʷpspuʷn/ **42**-13
south /saʊθ/ **9**
South /saʊθ/ **9**
South Africa /saʊθ ˈæfrɪkə/ **8**
South America
 /ˌsaʊθ əˈmɛrɪkə/ **7**
South Carolina
 /ˌsaʊθ kærəˈlaɪnə/ **9**
South China Sea
 /ˌsaʊθ tʃaɪnə ˈsiʸ/ **8**
South Dakota /ˌsaʊθ dəˈkoʷtə/ **9**
Southern States
 /ˌsʌðərn ˈsteʸts/ **9**
South Korea /ˌsaʊθ kəˈriʸə/ **8**
Southwest /ˌsaʊθ ˈwɛst/ **9**
Southwestern States
 /ˌsaʊθˌwɛstərn ˈsteʸts/ **9**
space /speʸs/ **77**
space shuttle /ˈspeʸs ˌʃʌtl/
 77-14
space suit /ˈspeʸs ˌsuʷt/ **77**-9
spaghetti /spəˈgɛtiʸ/ **17**-13
Spain /speʸn/ **8**
spatula /ˈspætʃələ/ **46**-31
speaker /ˈspiʸkər/ **51**-12
spectator /ˈspɛkteʸtər/ **65**-17
spectator sports
 /ˈspɛkteʸtər ˌsports/ **65**
speed limit sign
 /ˈspiʸd ˌlɪmɪt ˌsaɪn/ **58**-31
speedometer /spɪˈdamətər/
 55-14
sphere /sfɪər/ **5**-1
spice rack /ˈspaɪs ˌræk/ **45**-2
spices /ˈspaɪsɪz/ **45**-3

spider /ˈspaɪdər/ **76**-12
spinach /ˈspɪnɪtʃ/ **16**-18
spiral /ˈspaɪrəl/ **5**-23
spiral notebook
 /ˌspaɪrəl ˈnoʷtbʊk/ **80**-19
sponge /spʌndʒ/ **49**-14
sponge mop /ˈspʌndʒ ˌmap/
 49-10
sport coat /ˈsport ˌkoʷt/ **35**-9
sport jacket /ˈsport ˌdʒækɪt/
 35-9
sport shirt /ˈsport ˌʃɜrt/ **35**-13
spot /spat/ **71**-7
spotlight /ˈspatlaɪt/ **69**-16
spring /sprɪŋ/ **4**-4
square /ˈskwɛər/ **5**-D; **50**-23
squash /skwaʃ/ **68**-N
squash ball /ˈskwaʃ ˌbɔl/ **68**-48
squash player
 /ˈskwaʃ ˌpleʸər/ **68**-46
squash racket
 /ˈskwaʃ ˌrækɪt/ **68**-47
squirrel /ˈskwɜrəl/ **76**-15
Sri Lanka /sriʸ ˈlaŋkə/ **8**
stadium /ˈsteʸdiʸəm/ **65**-1
stadium lights
 /ˈsteʸdiʸəm ˌlaɪts/ **65**-2
stage /steʸdʒ/ **69**-13
stamp /stæmp/ **19**-18; **79**-8
stamp album /ˈstæmp ˌælbəm/
 79-7
stamp catalog
 /ˈstæmp ˌkætlˌɔg/ **79**-9
stamp collecting
 /ˈstæmp kəˌlɛktɪŋ/ **79**-6
stamp machine
 /ˈstæmp məˌʃiʸn/ **19**-10
stand /stænd/ **28**-21
staple /ˈsteʸpəl/ **20**-30
stapler /ˈsteʸplər/ **20**-10
star /stɑr/ **77**-2
starboard /ˈstɑrbərd/ **61**-5
starfish /ˈstɑrˌfɪʃ/ **74**-27
stationery /ˈsteʸʃəˌnɛriʸ/ **20**-14
station wagon
 /ˈsteʸʃən ˌwægən/ **55**-37
stay /steʸ/ **38**-21
steak /steʸk/ **14**-25; **17**-6
steering wheel /ˈstɪərɪŋ ˌhwiʸl/
 55-11
steps /stɛps/ **39**-19
stereo system
 /ˈstɛriʸoʷ ˌsɪstəm/ **51**-6
stern /stɜrn/ **61**-7
stethoscope /ˈstɛθəˌskoʷp/ **29**-2
stick /stɪk/ **66**-55
stirrup /ˈstɜrəp/ **67**-12
stomach /ˈstʌmək/ **23**-10
stomachache /ˈstʌmək̩eʸk/
 29-19
stop sign /ˈstap ˌsaɪn/ **58**-27
stork /stɔrk/ **75**-5
stormy /ˈstɔrmiʸ/ **4**-11
stove /stoʷv/ **45**-13
straight /streʸt/ **33**-23; **34**-37
straight pin /ˈstreʸt ˌpɪn/ **80**-10
strainer /ˈstreʸnər/ **46**-25
straw /strɔ/ **18**-21
strawberries /ˈstrɔˌbɛriʸz/ **15**-20
stream /striʸm/ **54**-15
street /striʸt/ **11**-9; **58**-22
street corner /ˌstriʸt ˈkɔrnər/
 11-13
street light /ˈstriʸt ˌlaɪt/ **12**-22;
 57-17
street sign /ˈstriʸt ˌsaɪn/ **12**-24

stretch /strɛtʃ/ **27**-2
string /strɪŋ/ **80**-31
string beans /ˈstrɪŋ biʸnz/ **16**-21
strings /strɪŋz/ **70**-A
stripe /straɪp/ **71**-18
striped /straɪpt/ **25**-32
stroller /ˈstroʷlər/ **47**-11
stuffed animal /ˌstʌft ˈænəməl/ **47**-8
stuffed tomatoes /ˌstʌft təˈmeʸtoʷz/ **17**-10
submarine /ˈsʌbməˌriʸn/ **78**-18
submarine sandwich /ˌsʌbməriʸn ˈsændwɪtʃ/ **18**-1
subway /ˈsʌbweʸ/ **12**-20
subway entrance /ˈsʌbweʸˌentrəns/ **12**-20
Sudan /suˈdæn/ **8**
suit /suʷt/ **35**-A, 1; **36**-A, 1
suitcase /ˈsuʷtkeʸs/ **56**-13; **59**-3
summer /ˈsʌmər/ **4**-1
Sun /sʌn/ **77**-4
Sunday /ˈsʌndiʸ/ **3**
sundries /ˈsʌndriʸz/ **80**-B
sunfish /ˈsʌnˌfɪʃ/ **74**-10
sun hat /ˈsʌn hæt/ **62**-15
sunny /ˈsʌniʸ/ **4**-5
supermarket /ˈsuʷpərˌmarkɪt/ **13**
surf /sɜrf/ **63**-15
surfboard /ˈsɜrfˌbɔrd/ **63**-16
surfer /ˈsɜrfər/ **63**-14
surfing /ˈsɜrfɪŋ/ **63**-F
Suriname /ˈsʊərəˌnam/ **7**
surprised /sərˈpraɪzd/ **32**-4
suspicious /səˈspɪʃəs/ **32**-25
swallow /ˈswaloʷ/ **75**-28
swan /swan/ **75**-4
Swaziland /ˈswaziʸlænd/ **8**
sweater /ˈswɛtər/ **35**-11
sweaters /ˈswɛtərz/ **37**-C
sweatshirt /ˈswɛt-ʃɜrt/ **36**-11
Sweden /ˈswiʸdn/ **8**
sweep /swiʸp/ **26**-15
sweet potatoes /ˈswiʸt pəˌteʸtoʷz/ **16**-13; **17**-12
swimmer /ˈswɪmər/ **63**-1
swimming /ˈswɪmɪŋ/ **63**-A
swimming pool /ˈswɪmɪŋ ˌpuʷl/ **63**-2
swing /swɪŋ/ **27**-9; **48**-5
switchboard /ˈswɪtʃbɔrd/ **20**-20
Switzerland /ˈswɪtsərlənd/ **8**
symphony /ˈsɪmfəniʸ/ **69**-A
Syria /ˈsɪriʸə/ **8**

table /ˈteʸbəl/ **40**-10; **42**-7; **68**-43
table tennis /ˈteʸbəl ˌtɛnɪs/ **68**-L
tail /teʸl/ **60**-40; **71**-5; **72**-47; **74**-4; **75**-23
taillight /ˈteʸlˌlaɪt/ **55**-9
tailor /ˈteʸlər/ **22**-42
Taiwan /ˌtaɪˈwan/ **8**
take /teʸk/ **28**-5
take a bath /ˌteʸk ə ˈbæθ/ **26**-19
take a shower /ˌteʸk ə ˈʃaʊər/ **26**-3
tall /tɔl/ **33**-13
tan /tæn/ **35**-26
tank /tæŋk/ **63**-9; **78**-9
tanker /ˈtæŋkər/ **61**-16
Tanzania /ˌtænzəˈniʸə/ **8**
tape /teʸp/ **20**-9; **51**-20; **52**-30
tape deck /ˈteʸp dɛk/ **51**-11
tape dispenser

tape dispenser /ˈteʸp dɪˌspɛnsər/ **20**-8
tape measure /ˈteʸp ˌmɛʒər/ **50**-13; **80**-3
tape recorder /ˈteʸp rɪˌkɔrdər/ **51**-17
target /ˈtargɪt/ **67**-16
taxi /ˈtæksiʸ/ **56**-15
taxi stand /ˈtæksiʸ ˌstænd/ **56**-C
tea /tiʸ/ **17**-24
teach /tiʸtʃ/ **28**-2
teacher /ˈtiʸtʃər/ **22**-35
teapot /ˈtiʸpat/ **42**-19
tear up /ˌtɛər ˈʌp/ **28**-6
teaspoon /ˈtiʸspuʷn/ **42**-14
teddy bear /ˈtɛdiʸ ˌbɛər/ **47**-7
teeter-totter /ˈtiʸtər ˌtatər/ **48**-1
telephone /ˈtɛləˌfoʷn/ **20**-20; **51**-22
telephone booth /ˈtɛləfoʷn ˌbuʷθ/ **11**-15
telephone sign /ˈtɛləfoʷn ˌsaɪn/ **58**-38
telescope /ˈtɛləˌskoʷp/ **79**-13
television /ˈtɛləˌvɪʒən/ **51**-4
teller /ˈtɛlər/ **6**-1; **22**-38
temperature /ˈtɛmpərətʃər/ **4**-C
temperature gauge /ˈtɛmpərətʃər ˌgeʸdʒ/ **55**-16
temple /ˈtɛmpəl/ **24**-41
Tennessee /ˌtɛnəˈsiʸ/ **9**
tennis /ˈtɛnɪs/ **66**-F
tennis ball /ˈtɛnɪs ˌbɔl/ **66**-59
tennis court /ˈtɛnɪs ˌkɔrt/ **66**-61
tennis player /ˈtɛnɪs ˌpleʸər/ **66**-57
tennis racket /ˈtɛnɪs ˌrækɪt/ **66**-58
tent /tɛnt/ **67**-27
tentacle /ˈtɛntəkəl/ **74**-13
terminal /ˈtɜrmənəl/ **59**-A; **60**-38
Texas /ˈtɛksəs/ **9**
Thailand /ˈtaɪlænd/ **8**
Thanksgiving /ˌθæŋksˈgɪvɪŋ/ **3**-12
theater /ˈθiʸətər/ **69**-D
thermometer /θərˈmamətər/ **29**-12
thick /θɪk/ **34**-41
thigh /θaɪ/ **23**-19
thimble /ˈθɪmbəl/ **80**-14
thin /θɪn/ **34**-42
third /θɜrd/ **1**
third base /ˌθɜrd ˈbeʸs/ **65**-14
third baseman /ˌθɜrd ˈbeʸsmæn/ **65**-12
thread /θrɛd/ **80**-13
three-pronged plug /ˌθriʸ prɔŋd ˈplʌg/ **49**-26
throat /θroʷt/ **24**-54
throw /θroʷ/ **27**-12
throw pillow /ˈθroʷ ˌpɪloʷ/ **41**-3; **43**-3
thumb /θʌm/ **23**-16
Thursday /ˈθɜrzdiʸ/ **3**
ticket /ˈtɪkɪt/ **59**-10
ticket agent /ˈtɪkɪt ˌeʸdʒənt/ **59**-1
ticket counter /ˈtɪkɪt ˌkaʊntər/ **56**-3; **59**-2
tie /taɪ/ **35**-7
tie bar /ˈtaɪ bar/ **38**-16
tie clip /ˈtaɪ klɪp/ **38**-16
tiepin /ˈtaɪpɪn/ **38**-15
tie rack /ˈtaɪtæk/ **38**-15
tiger /ˈtaɪgər/ **71**-3
tight /taɪt/ **33**-6

tight end /taɪt ɛnd/ **65**-31
tights /taɪts/ **36**-21
tile /taɪl/ **44**-4
time /taɪm/ **2**
times /taɪmz/ **1**
tire /taɪər/ **55**-35
tissue /ˈtɪʃuʷ/ **29**-14
tissue paper /ˈtɪʃuʷ ˌpeʸpər/ **80**-29
toaster /ˈtoʷstər/ **46**-21
toaster oven /ˈtoʷstər ˌʌvən/ **46**-19
toddler /ˈtadlər/ **48**-3
toe /toʷ/ **23**-23
toe shoe /ˈtoʷ ˌʃuʷ/ **69**-10
Togo /ˈtoʷgoʷ/ **8**
toilet /ˈtɔɪlɪt/ **44**-8
toilet paper /ˈtɔɪlɪt ˌpeʸpər/ **44**-13
toiletries /ˈtɔɪlətriʸz/ **25**-B
tollbooth /ˈtoʷlbuʷθ/ **57**-14
tollgate /ˈtoʷlgeʸt/ **57**-B
tomatoes /təˈmeʸtoʷz/ **16**-5
tomato juice /təˈmeʸtoʷ ˌdʒuʷs/ **17**-1
tongue /tʌŋ/ **24**-50
tool belt /ˈtuʷl ˌbɛlt/ **53**-6
toolbox /ˈtuʷlˌbaks/ **50**-1
tools /tuʷlz/ **50**
tooth /tuʷθ/ **24**-48; **30**-6
toothbrush /ˈtuʷθbrʌʃ/ **30**-11; **44**-17
toothbrush holder /ˈtuʷθbrʌʃ ˌhoʷldər/ **44**-18
toothpaste /ˈtuʷθpeʸst/ **30**-12
top /tap/ **5**-2; **47**-22
topaz /ˈtoʷpæz/ **38**-19
tortilla chips /tɔrˌtiʸə ˈtʃɪps/ **18**-12
tortise /ˈtɔrtəs/ **72**-34
tossed salad /ˌtɔst ˈsæləd/ **17**-5
tote bag /ˈtoʷt bæg/ **38**-26
touch /tʌtʃ/ **28**-17
towel /ˈtaʊəl/ **62**-5
towel rack /ˈtaʊəl ˌræk/ **44**-11
towrope /ˈtoʷroʷp/ **63**-23
track /træk/ **56**-6
tractor /ˈtræktər/ **73**-12
traffic /ˈtræfɪk/ **12**-19
traffic jam /ˈtræfɪk ˌdʒæm/ **12**-19
traffic light /ˈtræfɪk ˌlaɪt/ **11**-7; **58**-24
trail /treʸl/ **64**-9; **67**-25
train /treʸn/ **56**-5
train station /ˈtreʸn ˌsteʸʃən/ **56**-A
trash can /ˈtræʃ kæn/ **11**-4; **62**-6
traveler's check /ˈtrævələrz ˌtʃɛk/ **6**-16
tray /treʸ/ **30**-8; **60**-36
tray table /ˈtreʸ ˌteʸbəl/ **60**-35
tree /triʸ/ **40**-1; **54**-6
trench coat /ˈtrɛntʃ ˌkoʷt/ **37**-7
tricycle /ˈtraɪsɪkəl/ **48**-4
trivet /ˈtrɪvɪt/ **45**-5
trombone /tramˈboʷn/ **70**-7
tropical fish /ˌtrapɪkəl ˈfɪʃ/ **72**-53
trout /traʊt/ **74**-7
trowel /ˈtraʊəl/ **40**-18; **53**-16
truck /trʌk/ **57**-13
truck driver /ˈtrʌk ˌdraɪvər/ **21**-7
trumpet /ˈtrʌmpɪt/ **70**-10
trunk /trʌŋk/ **55**-7; **71**-10
trunks /trʌŋks/ **66**-68
t-shirt /ˈtiʸ ˌʃɜrt/ **35**-20; **36**-13
tub /tʌb/ **44**-5

tuba /ˈtuʷbə/ **70**-9
Tuesday /ˈtuzdiʸ/ **3**
tugboat /ˈtʌgboʷt/ **61**-19
tulip /ˈtuʷlɪp/ **40**-25
tuna fish /ˈtuʷnə ˌfɪʃ/ **14**-18
tuner /ˈtuʷnər/ **51**-10
tunnel /ˈtʌnl/ **57**-C
Turkey /ˈtɜrkiʸ/ **8**
turnips /ˈtɜrnɪps/ **16**-31
turn signal /ˈtɜrn ˌsɪgnəl/ **55**-17
turntable /ˈtɜrnˌteʸbəl/ **51**-8
turquoise /ˈtɜrkwɔɪz/ **38**-26
turtle /ˈtɜrtl/ **72**-37; **74**-20
turtleneck /ˈtɜrtlˌnɛk/ **37**-10
tusk /tʌsk/ **71**-9; **74**-19
TV /ˌtiʸ ˈviʸ/ **51**-4
two-family house /ˌtuʷ ˈfæməli ˌhaʊs/ **39**-C
two-story house /ˌtuʷ ˈstɔriʸ ˌhaʊs/ **39**-A
typewriter /ˈtaɪpˌraɪtər/ **20**-6
typing paper /ˈtaɪpɪŋ ˌpeʸpər/ **20**-7

Uganda /yʊˈgændə/ **8**
ugly /ˈʌgliʸ/ **33**-20
umbrella /ʌmˈbrɛlə/ **37**-6; **40**-9; **62**-8
umpire /ˈʌmpaɪər/ **65**-16
uncle /ˈʌŋkəl/ **31**
under /ˈʌndər/ **34**-48
underpants /ˈʌndərˌpænts/ **36**-17
underpass /ˈʌndərˌpæs/ **57**-2
undershirt /ˈʌndərˌʃɜrt/ **35**-20
underwear /ˈʌndərˌwɛər/ **35**-C; **36**-C
uniform /ˈyuʷnəˌfɔrm/ **65**-22
Union of Soviet Socialist Republics /ˌyuʷnyən əv ˌsoʷviʸət ˌsoʷʃəlɪst rɪˈpʌblɪks/ **8**
United Arab Emirates /yuʷˌnaɪtɪd ˌærəb əˈmɪərɪts/ **8**
United States /yuˌnaɪtɪd ˈsteʸts/ **7**; **9**
upper arm /ˌʌpər ˈarm/ **23**-28
Upper Volta /ˌʌpər ˈvoʷltə/ **8**
upstairs apartment /ˌʌpstɛərz əˈpartmənt/ **39**-16
Uruguay /ˈyʊərəgwaɪ/ **7**
Utah /ˈyuʷtə/ **9**
utility knife /yuʷˈtɪlətiʸ ˌnaɪf/ **50**-8

vacuum cleaner /ˈvækyuʷm ˌkliʸnər/ **49**-9
Valentine's Day /ˈvæləntaɪnz ˌdeʸ/ **3**-2
valley /ˈvæliʸ/ **54**-4
van /væn/ **57**-10
vase /veʸs/ **41**-18
VCR /ˌviʸ siʸ ˈar/ **51**-1
vegetable field /ˈvɛdʒtəbəl ˌfiʸld/ **73**-10
vegetable garden /ˈvɛdʒtəbəl ˌgardn/ **40**-15
vegetables /ˈvɛdʒtəbəlz/ **16**
vein /veʸn/ **24**-53
Venezuela /ˌvɛnəˈzweʸlə/ **7**
Vermont /vərˈmant/ **9**
vest /vɛst/ **35**-8
veterinarian /ˌvɛtərəˈneəriʸən/ **22**-30
Victoria Island /ˌvɪkˈtɔriʸə ˌaɪlənd/ **10**

video camera /ˈvɪdiˠoʷ ˌkæmərə/ **52**-43
video cassette /ˌvɪdiˠoʷ kəˈsɛt/ **51**-2
video cassette recorder /ˌvɪdiˠoʷ kəˈsɛt rɪˌkɔrdər/ **51**-1
Vietnam /ˌviˠɛtˈnam/ **8**
viola /viˠˈoʷlə/ **70**-3
violin /ˌvaɪəˈlɪn/ **70**-2
Virginia /vərˈdʒɪnyə/ **9**
vise /vaɪs/ **50**-21
V-neck /viˠ nɛk/ **37**-11
vocalist /ˈvoʷkəlɪst/ **69**-21
volleyball /ˈvaliˠbɔl/ **68**-1, 29
volleyball player /ˈvaliˠbɔl ˌpleˠər/ **68**-28
voltage converter /ˈvoʷltɪdʒ kənˌvɜrtər/ **52**-33

wading pool /ˈweˠdɪŋ ˌpuʷl/ **40**-6
waist /weˠst/ **23**-30
waiter /ˈweˠtər/ **21**-22
waiting room /ˈweˠtɪŋ ˌruʷm/ **59**-9
waitress /ˈweˠtrəs/ **21**-23
wake up /ˌweˠk ˈʌp/ **26**-1
walk /wɔk/ **27**-6
Walkman /ˈwɔkmən/ **51**-18
walk sign /ˈwɔk ˌsaɪn/ **11**-16
wallet /ˈwalət/ **38**-29
wall socket /ˈwɔl ˌsakɪt/ **49**-27
wall unit /ˈwɔl ˌyuʷnɪt/ **41**-10
walrus /ˈwɔlrəs/ **74**-18
warm /wɔrm/ **4**-b
wash your face /ˌwaʃ yər ˈfeˠs/ **26**-8
washcloth /ˈwaʃklɔθ/ **44**-27
washer /ˈwaʃər/ **49**-15; **50**-6
washing machine /ˈwaʃɪŋ məˌʃiˠn/ **49**-15
Washington /ˈwaʃɪŋtən/ **9**
wastepaper basket /ˈweˠst ˌpeˠpər ˌbæskɪt/ **20**-15
watch /watʃ/ **2**-e, f; **26**-17; **38**-2
watch TV /ˌwatʃ ˌtiˠ ˈviˠ/ **26**-17
water /ˈwɔtər/ **54**
watercress /ˈwɔtərˌkrɛs/ **16**-4
waterfall /ˈwɔtərˌfɔl/ **54**-16
water fountain /ˈwɔtər ˌfaʊntn/ **48**-14
waterfront /ˈwɔtərˌfrʌnt/ **61**
water glass /ˈwɔtər ˌglæs/ **42**-3
watering can /ˈwɔtərɪŋ ˌkæn/ **40**-16
watermelons /ˈwɔtərˌmɛlənz/ **15**-23
Water Pik /ˈwɔtər ˌpɪk/ **30**-15
water ski /ˈwɔtər ˌskiˠ/ **63**-22
water-skier /ˈwɔtər ˌskiˠər/ **63**-21
waterskiing /ˈwɔtərˌskiˠɪŋ/ **63**-1
water sports /ˈwɔtər ˌspɔrts/ **63**
wave /weˠv/ **28**-20; **62**-12
weather /ˈwɛðər/ **4**-B
weaving /ˈwiˠvɪŋ/ **79**-19
Wednesday /ˈwɛnzdiˠ/ **3**
week /wiˠk/ **3**-C
welder /ˈwɛldər/ **21**-9
west /wɛst/ **9**
West Coast /ˌwɛst ˈkoʷst/ **9**
Western Canada /ˌwɛstərn ˈkænədə/ **10**
Western Sahara /ˌwɛstərn səˈhærə/ **8**
West Germany /ˌwɛst ˈdʒɜrməniˠ/ **8**

West Virginia /ˌwɛst vərˈdʒɪnyə/ **9**
wet /wɛt/ **33**-21
wet mop /ˈwɛt ˌmap/ **49**-12
wet suit /ˈwɛt suʷt/ **63**-8
whale /ˈweˠl/ **74**-14
wheat field /ˈhwiˠt ˌfiˠld/ **73**-8
wheel /hwiˠl/ **67**-7
wheelbarrow /ˈhwiˠlˌbæroʷ/ **53**-19
whisk /hwɪsk/ **46**-28
whisk broom /ˈhwɪsk ˌbruʷm/ **49**-6
whiskers /ˈhwɪskərz/ **72**-43
white /hwaɪt/ **35**-24
white water rafting /ˌhwaɪt ˌwɔtər ˈræftɪŋ/ **63**-M
wide /waɪd/ **34**-39
wide receiver /ˌwaɪd rɪˈsiˠvər/ **65**-30, 38
width /wɪdθ/ **5**-14
wife /waɪf/ **31**
winch /wɪntʃ/ **61**-11
window /ˈwɪndoʷ/ **39**-8; **41**-13; **60**-30
window seat /ˈwɪndoʷ ˌsiˠt/ **60**-31
window washer /ˈwɪndoʷ ˌwaʃər/ **21**-5
windshield /ˈwɪndʃiˠld/ **55**-6
windshield wiper /ˈwɪndʃiˠld ˌwaɪpər/ **55**-12
windsurfer /ˈwɪndˌsɜrfər/ **63**-17
windsurfing /ˈwɪndˌsɜrfɪŋ/ **63**-G
windy /ˈwɪndiˠ/ **4**-13
wine glass /ˈwaɪn ˌglæs/ **42**-2
wing /wɪŋ/ **60**-42; **75**-27
winter /ˈwɪntər/ **4**-3
winter sports /ˌwɪntər ˈspɔrts/ **64**
Wisconsin /wɪˈskansɪn/ **9**
withdrawal slip /wɪðˈdrɔəl ˌslɪp/ **6**-12
women's wear /ˈwɪmɪnz ˌwɛər/ **36**; **37**
woodwinds /ˈwʊdˌwɪndz/ **70**-C
woodworking /ˈwʊdˌwɜrkɪŋ/ **79**-25
workbench /ˈwɜrkbɛntʃ/ **50**-22
world /wɜrld/ **7**
worried /ˈwɜriˠd/ **32**-17
wrapping paper /ˈræpɪŋ ˌpeˠpər/ **80**-26
wrench /rɛntʃ/ **50**-9
wrestler /ˈrɛslər/ **66**-63
wrestling /ˈrɛslɪŋ/ **66**-G
wrist /rɪst/ **23**-13
write /raɪt/ **28**-1
Wyoming /waɪˈoʷmɪŋ/ **9**

Xerox machine /ˈzɪərɑks məˌʃiˠn/ **20**-31
x-ray /ˈɛks reˠ/ **29**-5
x-ray machine /ˈɛks reˠ məˌʃiˠn/ **30**-5
xylophone /ˈzaɪləˌfoʷn/ **70**-19

yard /yɑrd/ **5**-25
yard stick /ˈyɑrdˌstɪk/ **5**-24
yarn /yɑrn/ **80**-4
year /yɪər/ **3**-A
yellow /ˈyɛloʷ/ **36**-23
yellow peppers /ˌyɛloʷ ˈpɛpərz/ **16**-8

Yemen (Aden) /ˈyɛmən/ (/ˈeˠdn/) **8**
Yemen (Sana) /ˈyɛmən/ (/ˈsanə/) **8**
yield sign /ˈyiˠld ˌsaɪn/ **58**-28
yogurt /ˈyoʷgərt/ **13**-12
young /yʌŋ/ **33**-15
Yugoslavia /ˌyuʷgoʷˈslaviˠə/ **8**
Yukon Territory /ˈyuʷkən ˌtɛrətɔriˠ/ **10**

Zaire /zɑˈɪər/ **8**
Zambia /ˈzæmbiˠə/ **8**
zebra /ˈziˠbrə/ **71**-17
Zimbabwe /zɪmˈbabwiˠ/ **8**
zip code /ˈzɪp koʷd/ **19**-17
zipper /ˈzɪpər/ **80**-7
zoo /zuʷ/ **71**-A

Los créditos de foto incluyen a todos los que han contribuido al *Diccionario Fotográfico Longman*. Los números en negrita aluden a la página en que la fotografía o contribución aparece; los números entre prantesis se refieren a la fotografía.

A & M Records, Inc. **69** (21)
AAA **57** (1–4)
AAU/USA Junior Olympics **66** (40–43)
Alaska Division of Tourism **54** (15)
Alcoa **39** (1–11)
Ethan Allen **42** (excluding inset)
American Airlines **59** (12–17); **60** (22–33)
American Institute of Baking **21** (20)
American Cyanamid Company **76** (5)
Copyright by the American Dental Association. Reprinted by Permission. **22** (28)
American Egg Board **13** (14)
American Motors **55** (11–19, 23–24, 36, 38)
American Optometric Association **22** (29)
American Trucking Associations **57** (5–13)
(C) AMPS, 1984. **63** (3–4, 28–35); **64** (2–12, 16–17); **66** (48–56, 63–64, 66–71); **67** (13–16)
Aristokraft **45** (1–25)
Armour Processed Meat Company **18** (1)
(C) Art Attack, 1986. **12** (22–28)
Art Students League of New York. Photos by Mitchell Cherry. **22** (46); **79** (23–24)
Guy F. Atkinson Company of California. Photos by Ron Chamberlain. **21** (1); **53** (2–6)
Australian Information Service **71** (26–27)
Australian Tourist Commission **71** (25); **75** (2–3)
Ministry of Tourism, Bahamas **63** (19–20), **74** (21)
Baker's German Sweet Chocolate **17** (20)
Baldwin **70** (20)
Bank of America **6** (1–5); **22** (38)
Bechtel Power Corporation **53** (7)
Bethlehem Steel Corporation **53** (10–11)
The Bettmann Archive **33** (11–12)
Gerard Bollei **22** (40)
Boston Symphony Orchestra **69** (3–5)
E. J. Brach & Sons **3** (2)
Douglas Brkich **2** (g–j); **68** (49–52)
Jules Bucher **4** (7); **77** (7)
Van Bucher **4** (6); **11** (3–5, 7–18); **12** (20–21); **13** (9–12, 16–17); **14** (20, 22–24, F, 27–28); **15**; **16**; **17** (1, 22); **18** (6–10, 13, 15, 17–18); **21** (5–6, 13, 22); **22** (25); **30** (13, 17–18); **34** (33–36, 39–41); **39** (20); **44** (9–21); **45** (31); **48**; **54** (5–8); **56** (1–4, 11–14); **58** (20–23); **69** (19–20); **75** (21); **79** (6–11, 14, 17–18)
Bumble Bee Seafoods, Inc. **14** (18)
W. Atlee Burpee Co. **40** (14, 16–26)
California Avocado Commission **17** (5)
Campbell Soup Co. **14** (19); **17** (4)
Canadian Pacific Ltd. **56** (5–10)
Carolina Biological Supply Company **24** (51–61)
Caulk Dentsply **30** (6)
Cayman Islands Department of Tourism **63** (5–6)
CBS News **22** (32)
Charles River Lab, Inc. **76** (14)
Chase Manhattan Archives **22** (34, 37)
Chock Full o' Nuts **17** (23); **34** (27)
Ciba-Geigy **22** (24)
Citibank **6** (8); **11** (1); **12** (19); **22** (36); **53** (12–13)
City of Chicago Department of Aviation **59** (5–6)
Clairol **33** (23–24)
Bruce Coleman, Inc. **4** (5) photo © Wendell Metzen; **22** (43) photo by S.L. Craig, Jr.; **34** (25) photo by M.P. Kahl; **53** (1) photo © Wendell Metzen; **69** (16–18) photo © Michael S. Rewner; **72** (41–43) photo by Franklin J. Sanborn
Colgate-Palmolive Company **30** (12)

Cornell Laboratory of Ornithology **75** (12) photo by Allen Cruickshank; (22–23) photo by W.R. Spafford; (24–25) photos by Mike Hopiak; (28) photo by John S. Dunning
CPC International **13** (15); **14** (31)
(C) David J. Cross, 1986. **75** (1)
Dairy Goat Journal **73** (26–27)
Department of the Army **78** (1–9)
Ducks Unlimited, Inc. **75** (8–9)
Edmund Scientific Company **79** (12–13)
Harvey Eisner **21** (12)
Evenflo Juvenile Furniture Company **47** (12–13, 16)
FACT **13** (B)
Fashion Institute of Technology **22** (44–45) photo by John Senzer
Fieldcrest **43** (19–20)
Fine Woodworking **79** (25)
Florida Division of Tourism **62** (19–20); **63** (17–18, 25–27); **67** (17–21); **71** (3–5, 13–14, 24); **72** (32, 37)
Ford **55** (37)
Frito-Lay, Inc. **18** (11–12)
Gaines Dog Care Center **72** (38–40)
Gerber Products Company **47** (1–11, 14–15, 17–24)
Godfather's Pizza **18** (3)
The Great Eastern Mussel Farms, Inc. **74** (23)
Haagen-Dazs **17** (21)
Hallmark Cards **3** (1, 5–6, 11–13)
The Handweavers Guild of America **79** (19–20) photo by Hodges Glenn, Jr.
Hawaii Vistors Bureau **63** (14–16)
Grant Heilman **73** (29–30); **75** (19–20)
Hershey **18** (16)
Highway Users Federation **58** (18–19, 26–39)
H.U.D. **39** (25–31)
Hohner, Inc. **70** (21–22)
Houston Grand Opera **69** (6–7) photo by Jim Caldwell
Indiana University **65** (27–38)
International Numismatic Society **79** (1–5)
Ireland-Gannon Associates, Inc. **39** (12–14); **40** (8–13); **79** (21–22)
Japan National Tourist Organization **34** (42); **66** (65); **79** (21–22)
Joseph R. Jehl, Jr. **75** (10–11, 29–30)
George E. Joseph **69** (11–15)
Kansas City International Airport **59** (7–9, 18–20); **60** (38–43)
John F. Kennedy Library **31** (A, G)
Kenya Tourist Office **54** (16); **63** (1–2); **71** (11–12, 21); **72** (35); **75** (13)
Kick Enterprises **66** (44–47)
Aaron Kiley **55** (25–32)
Kimberly Clark Corporation **47** (25)
Kraft, Inc. **13** (13)
(C) James R. Levin, 1986. **44** (1–8)
Thomas J. Lipton, Inc. **34** (28)
(C) Los Angeles Dodgers, Inc. 1985. **65** (19–26)
Macy's **3** (12); **41**
Marriott Corporation **18** (2, 5)
Maybelline **24** (37–38)
Metropolitan Transportation Authority **57** (15, 17)
Miami Seaquarium **74** (9, 15–17)
Milton Bradley Company **79** (29)
Milwaukee Symphony Orchestra **69** (1–2)
Ji H. Min **44** (22–27)
Monkmeyer Press **21** (11) photo by Paul Conklin; **22** (39) photo by David Conklin, (42) photo by Hugh Rogers; **34** (47–48) photo by Jason Horowitz ©1985; **53** (20) photo by Hugh Rogers
Benjamin Moore **21** (4)
Murray Chris-Craft Cruisers, Inc. **63** (21–24)
Nabisco Brands, Inc. **14** (29–30)
NASA **77** (1–3, 5–6, 8–17)
National Aquarium **74** (10, 12–14, 22, 27)
National Association of Women in Construction **53** (19)
National Bowling Council **68** (34–38)
National Broiler Council **17** (14–16)

National Cattlemen's Association **73** (23)
National 4-H Council **73** (10–14)
National Live Stock and Meat Board **17** (6–13)
National Marine Fisheries Service **4** (9–10); **21** (15); **63** (7–10); **74** (1–4, 11, 18–20, 26)
National Park Service **4** (3, 8); **54** (9–12, 17–18); **64** (18); **72** (36); **74** (24–25); **75** (14–15); **76** (16)
Joseph Nettis **21** (23)
New England Shrimp Company **17** (3)
N.J. Travel and Tourism **4** (1)
New York Convention & Vistors Bureau **3** (9); **58** (D); **65** (1–17); **66** (72)
New York Public Library Picture Collection **3** (3)
New Zealand Lamb Company, Inc. **14** (26)
NOAA **4** (11–13)
(C) Aaron Norman, 1986. **58** (24–25); **71** (19–20, 28); **72** (51–53); **76** (7, 9, 11–12, 15)
North Atlantic Seafood Association **17** (17–18)
Ovation Instruments, Inc. **70** (6)

Parker Brothers **79** (31)
The Popcorn Institute **18** (14)
Port Authority of N.Y. and N.J. **21** (8, 10); **53** (9); **56** (15–19); **59** (4); **60** (44–47); **61** (1–7, 20)
Port of Houston Authority **61** (8–13, 17–19)
Port of New Orleans **61** (16)
Portland Cement Association **21** (2); **53** (14–15)
Pressman Toy Corporation **79** (28)
Produce Marketing Association **21** (18)
Red Lobster **18** (4)
R. J. Reynolds Industries, Inc. **13** (1–8); **14** (D); **45** (28–29)
Rhythm Band Inc. **70** (12)
(C) Safeway Stores, Inc. 1986 **13** (C); **14** (E)
Salt Lake Valley Convention & Visitors Bureau **69** (8–10)
O. M. Scott & Sons Company **40** (1–6, 15)
Sealy, Incorporated **43** (21–22)
Seaman Furniture Company, Inc. **43** (1–13)
Selchow & Righter **79** (30)
The Selmer Company **70** (1–5, 7–11, 13–19)
Arthur Shay **68** (46–48)
Shell Oil Company **55** (1–10)
The Singer Company **80** (1)
SK, Inc. **11** (6); **39** (15–19, 22–24)
Smithsonian Institution **71** (1–2, 6–10, 17–18); **72** (33–34)
Society of American Florists **21** (17)
St. Charles Manufacturing Co. **45** (26–27, 30)
Stock, Boston **24** (50) photo by Mike Mazzaschi
Sunkist **17** (2)
Swiss National Tourist Office **54** (1–4); **67** (22–25)
Tea Council of the U.S.A., Inc. **17** (24)
Teledyne Water Pik **30** (15)
Julie Betts Testwuide **67** (2)
Frank Teti **31** (B–F, H–O)
Tourist Development Division, City of Virginia Beach **62** (1–13)

Trammell Crow Company **53** (8, 16–18)
Transport Workers Union of America **3** (10)
TWA **59** (1–3); **60** (34–37)
UN Photo **33** (15–16); **77** (4)
U.S. Air Force Photo **3** (7); **78** (10–13, 15–16)
U.S. Chess Federation **79** (26–27)
U.S. Navy Photo **78** (14, 17–22, D)
USDA **4** (4); **14** (21, 25); **21** (9, 16, 19); **22** (41); **54** (13–14); **61** (14–15); **73** (1–9, 15–22, 24–25); **75** (31–32); **76** (1–4, 6, 8, 10); **79** (15–16)
U.S. Fish and Wildlife Service **34** (26); **71** (15–16, 22–23, 29–31); **72** (50); **74** (5–8); **75** (4–7, 16–18, 26–27)
United States Amateur Confederation of Roller Skating **68** (31–33)
United States Handball Association **68** (44–45)
The United States Playing Card Company **79** (32)
United States Pony Clubs, Inc. **67** (8–12)
United States Postal Service **21** (14)
USA Volleyball Team **68** (28–30)
United States Table Tennis Association. Photo (C) Robert Compton. **68** (39–43)
Utah Travel Council **64** (13–15)
Louise B. Van der Meid **72** (44–49)
Van Waters & Rogers **76** (13)
Vermont Travel Division **4** (2); **64** (1)
Via Rail Canada **56** (8–10)
Virginia Division of Tourism **62** (14–18); **67** (1, 3–7, 26–27)
Volvo Cars of North America **55** (33–35)
Warner-Lambert Co. **30** (14)
Wells Fargo Bank **6** (6–7)
Western New York Apple Growers Association, Inc. **17** (19)
White House Photo **22** (33)
Woodfin Camp & Associates **21** (3, 7) photos by John Blaustein, (21) photo by William Hubbell; **22** (30–31) photos by Michal Heron
World Championship Tennis **66** (57–62)
Xerox **20** (31)

Contributors

We would like to thank the following establishments for their cooperation:

Bloomingdale's, White Plains, New York **42** (10–14)
Charles Librett Hardware, New Rochelle, New York **50**; **53** (21–23)
Daminc Jewelers, New York, New York **2**(f)
The Family Medical Group of Manhattan, New York, New York **29** (1–8)
Farrington Square Apothecary, White Plains, New York **33** (19–20)
Kinney Shoes, White Plains, New York **37** (13–21)
Mamaroneck Post Office, Mamaroneck, New York **19** (1–9)
Nathan's, Yonkers, New York **18** (19–27)
Newmark and Lewis, Scarsdale, New York **51** (6–12)
Riverdale Country School, Riverdale, New York **22** (35); **28**
Sears Roebuck and Co., White Plains, New York **43** (14–18)
YMCA, White Plains, New York **27**

Special thanks to April Cicero and David Godsey for their creativity and talent (cover and page **32**), and to all the models who volunteered their time, energy and patience.

ACKNOWLEDGEMENTS
AGRADECIMIENTOS

Queremos agradecer en particular a:

☐ *Carol Taylor* y *Arley Gray* por darse cuenta del potencial de la obra;

☐ *Joanne Dresner,* nuestra editora, por su paciencia, perseverancia, excelente juicio y buen humor;

☐ *Penny Laporte,* editora del proyecto, por su amplio esfuerzo y atención a los pormenores;

☐ *Joseph DePinho* por la creatividad de su diseño;

☐ *Stella Kupferberg,* por su inagotable energía, habilidad y paciencia para encontrar la fotografía perfecta;

☐ *Irwin Feigenbaum,* por su talento gramatical;

☐ *John Rosenthal, Ann Rosenthal* y *Peter Freeman* por sus consejos y participación;

☐ *Melody Miller* de la oficina del senador Kennedy, por su amabilidad y estímulo;

☐ *Frank Teti,* por sus espléndidas fotografías de la familia Kennedy;

☐ *Barbara Swartz,* por sus excepcionales cualidades para escuchar;

y

a los profesores y estudiantes de todo el mundo que esperamos disfruten de la selección de vocabulario y fotografías de nuestra cultura tanto como nosotros.

Longman Group UK Ltd
Longman House
Burnt Mill
Harlow, Essex CM20 2JE
Copyright © Longman Group UK Ltd. 1990

British Library Cataloguing in Publication Data
Rosenthal, Marilyn S.
Longman Photo Dictionary
1. English language – Dictionaries for non-English speaking students
I. Title II. Freeman, Daniel B, 1920–423
ISBN 0 582 08011.8

Printed in USA.